CHANAKYA NEETI

STRATEGIES *for* SUCCESS

RADHAKRISHNAN PILLAI

JAICO PUBLISHING HOUSE

Ahmedabad Bangalore Bhopal Chennai
Delhi Hyderabad Kolkata Lucknow Mumbai

Published by Jaico Publishing House
A-2 Jash Chambers, 7-A Sir Phirozshah Mehta Road
Fort, Mumbai - 400 001
jaicopub@jaicobooks.com
www.jaicobooks.com

CHANAKYA NEETI
ISBN 978-93-88423-57-1

First Jaico Impression: 2020
Second Jaico Impression: 2020

All quoted verses are based on
Chanakya's Neeti Scripture by R. K. Sharma
published by Bharatiya Vidya Bhavan,
K. M. Munshi Marg, Mumbai-400007
Copyright © R.K. Sharma
Used with the permission of Bharatiya Vidya Bhavan

Page design and layout: R. Ajith Kumar, Delhi

This book can tell you what to do and what not to do.
So let vivek shakti *(the power of intellect) rise in each of you.*
I dedicate this book to all great people who knew what
to do and what not to do in any given situation.
Those are the great men and women
who can each be truly called...
The Chanakya of their times.

CONTENTS

INTRODUCTION

The moment we hear the two words 'Chanakya Neeti', we're transported to another world, the world of Chanakya where there was order and discipline.

However, Chanakya Neeti can have various meanings for various people.

While Chanakya was a well-known figure in Indian history, not many people are familiar with the meaning of *neeti*.

In Sanskrit, *neeti* has many definitions—strategies, policies, ideas, principles, methods, plans or tactics.

But before we start discussing this book *Chanakya Neeti*, let's first try and understand Chanakya.

This great thinker, philosopher, statesman and political strategist lived in the fourth century BC and led a life that is worth studying. He was known by three names—Vishnugupta, Chanakya and Kautilya.

It is said that he was born with a full set of teeth, and that there was a prophecy which predicted that he will rule the country without occupying the seat of power. That is exactly what happened as his life unfolded.

His father was Chanak, who was a teacher of *rajaneeti* or political science. Chanak used to advise Dhanananda, the king of Magadha. However, Dhanananda was corrupt and people were unhappy with his leadership.

Chanak went on to create a public awakening, for which Dhanananda murdered him. Chanakya, then only a small boy, had to run away from Magadha to save his life. He reached Takshashila, and in Takshashila not only did he get a chance to survive but he continued his studies at the famous university. Chanakya was a brilliant student, and he soon became a teacher of political science, just like his father.

But destiny had other larger plans for him.

One day, he returned to Magadha, and Pataliputra, its capital, became his playground. He soon challenged Dhanananda and dethroned him.

He started training many young students in political science and leadership. He made one of his brightest students, Chandragutpa Maurya, the king of Magadha. Chanakya also defeated Alexander the Great, who was on his way to conquer the world.

Later, Chanakya brought together all the 16 regional kingdoms of India under one central government and thus established *Akhanda Bharat*—United India, and made Chandragupta its Emperor.

However, Chanakya was a teacher at his core. He wanted to pass on his wisdom and experiences to the next generation. He, therefore, wrote his magnum opus, *Kautilya's Arthashastra*—one of the greatest books ever written on leadership and good governance.

The *Arthashastra* has 6000 *sutras* or formulas based on which he guided Chandragupta on how to govern well. This book is still studied by scholars across the globe and our generation still derives guidance and inspiration from it.

Chanakya wrote the *Arthashastra* for kings and leaders. But what about the common man? Why would a teacher neglect the masses? He didn't. He wanted to guide the common man too.

Therefore, it is said that while the *Arthashastra* with its 6000 *sutras* was meant for kings, he wrote another book, *Chanakya Neeti*, for the common man. What is in your hands is this *Chanakya Neeti*.

There are many arguments about the origins of *Chanakya Neeti* — who wrote it, where, when, etc. Some scholars have said that it is the essence of the original *Arthashastra* modified for the common man while some others have debated that it was compiled by some students of Chanakya to distill the wisdom of the *Arthashastra* for the masses.

Whatever be the debate around *Chanakya Neeti*, it surely gives us in a concise manner what Chanakya wanted us to know. If you cannot study the full *Arthashastra*, I suggest that you at least start with *Chanakya Neeti*.

I am sure after reading this book you will be inspired to go through the 6000 *sutras* of the *Arthashastra*. I promise you that if you earnestly study these two books, your life will never be the same again; it will change for the better.

Now, about the book in your hands: the original *Chanakya Neeti* has many sources and there are various versions available across India. I am not a historian and it is difficult to find the original book as such. But after studying about 40 different versions, I have come to the conclusion that they are all more or less the same.

For easy reference, I have used the book *Chanakya's Neeti Scripture*, which is among the first verse-by-verse English translations available of the original Sanskrit text. This was done by the great scholar R.K. Sharma and it was published by Bharatiya Vidya Bhavan. My salutations to Mr. Sharma for his phenomenal work in translating each of Chanakya's ideas into simple English so that people around the world can read and enjoy them.

Writing this book has been one of my most difficult projects till date. I have written over 15 books on Chanakya in addition to research papers and other articles for magazines and newspapers. But writing commentary on each verse in this book was a challenge in itself.

How can a common man like me write a commentary on a great ancient scripture like *Chanakya Neeti*? Commentary or *bhashya* (in Sanskrit) is the privilege of great scholars. In the past you could write one on a *shastra* (scripture) like *Chanakya Neeti* only if you are an authority on the subject, and that too with other scholars' approvals.

So when I started writing my commentary on *Chanakya Neeti*, I remembered my lifelong guides to understand Chanakya's wisdom: Swami Tejomayananda and Swami Advayananda of the Chinmaya Mission; Dr. Gangadharan Nair and Dr. Shubhada Joshi—my teachers from the Chinmaya University and University of Mumbai respectively. They have been my constant source of inspiration.

The commentary you are about to read is based directly on Chanakya's original Sanskrit text, which was primarily written for male readers. He lived during a time where casteism and discrimination against women were considered normal. As a result, many of his original thoughts may seem outdated or outrageous in today's context. Chanakya's writing reflects the social practices prevalent in his lifetime. The idea behind this book is not to cause offence to any religion, caste, race, gender or place. I have tried my best to provide a modern take on all the verses you will come across in these pages, so that you get to understand them in a broader context. It's my sincere plea, dear reader, to keep these words in mind as you go through this book.

I would like to thank my publishers, Jaico Publishing House, for bringing out yet another milestone of a book on Chanakya through me. Akash Shah is more a friend than a publisher to me. I have yet to meet another great human being like him. Simple and profound, he has always been a constant support to me as an author ever since our first book, *Corporate Chanakya*. I would also like to thank the entire Jaico team for making this book possible.

A special mention to my student Jayesh Solanki who meticulously researched the original sources of *Chanakya Neeti*. He also helped me with the translation of each verse in this book. Jayesh has been a true research scholar throughout the process.

Also, thanks to my team—Nitya Somaiya, Pranav Patel, Karthiga Thevar, Nikhil Murari, Soumya Valeja and Surekha Pillai—who helps me with the ideation, editing and marketing of my books.

And finally, my sincere thanks to my wife, Surekha, and kids, Aanvikshiki and Arjun. As in my family, every family should try to read books from India's great and glorious past together, so that they learn and grow together.

One last thing…

For me, *Chanakya Neeti* means those methods that one can use to get one's 'desired results or outcomes.'

If you truly study and apply the *neetis* in this book in your life, you can easily achieve your life goals.

Best wishes for a successful life…

Dr. Radhakrishnan Pillai

CHAPTER 1

OPENING VERSES

1.1

Firstly, I bow my head to Vishnu
The preserver lord of the triple-world*
And enunciate the code of regal conduct
From numerous scriptures culled

India, as a nation, is unique, mostly because of its varied cultures and traditions. We always invoke divine blessings before starting anything new, irrespective of our caste or religion, in the belief that this prayerful gesture at the beginning of a project will help us carry it out successfully, and finish it without any obstruction. Similarly, Chanakya starts *Chanakya Neeti* by invoking Lord Vishnu. He writes: "First and foremost, I bow my head to Lord Vishnu." This is a sign of submission. Chanakya was a person of high intellect but he knew that one needs to surrender one's ego to God.

In Indian mythology, Vishnu is considered the sustainer, the lord of the three worlds—Earth, Heaven and the world below the Earth (called *Patal*). Praying for the blessings of Lord Vishnu, Chanakya proceeds to write the code of conduct that befits royals. This does not mean that *Chanakya Neeti* is only for kings and noblemen; it is equally useful to commoners like us who want to become royalty in our own fields through hardwork and by leading a dignified life. *Chanakya Neeti* is the essence of various scriptures Chanakya carefully studied to come up with a code of conduct that will benefit all mankind.

Invoke the lord

Usually people remember God only during hardships. But what if we seek God's help even before we embark on something important? If that's the case, then Chanakya assures us that our problems will not derail our progress.

---

* Of gods, men and demons

Swami Chinmayananda, the great spiritual master, suggested: "Remember God before you start, then the whole journey will become divine and you will never see any situation as a problem at all." This way, our lives will become spiritual in nature. We will not complain. In fact, we will have faith in the higher power, and with that faith all problems will cease to exist.

Become royals

Chanakya wrote *Chanakya Neeti* to lay down the rules of conduct or valuable lessons for those who are kings or want to be kings. After all, he was a kingmaker for the masses. He wrote *Arthashastra* for the ruling class; after all, he was a kingmaker. But he also sensed the need to have a set of guidelines for the common man to help him live a life of dignity and prosperity. As a result, *Chanakya Neeti* was born. Even poor people can have self-respect; even poor people can be righteous. Though from an ordinary background, through proper conduct, strength of character and refined behaviour anyone can lead a life equal to tthat of a king, shows *Chanakya Neeti*.

Never compromise your values for petty things. Stand up for your beliefs. That is the proper way to lead a dignified and regal life. Swami Tejomayananda said, "If you don't stand up for something, you will fall for everything."

The essence of great scriptures

Chanakya, a great scholar himself, studied various scriptures to research ideal conduct and moral codes. And he wrote a great one himself—*Arthashastra*. But the brilliance of Chanakya's wisdom is not in studying and writing scriptures, but in simplifying these complicated writings for practical application. He was able to provide the gist of all his knowledge in simple *sutras* or *neetis* (formulas). Therefore, this book, *Chanakya Neeti*, is the very essence of Chanakya's immense wisdom and all the ancient scriptures, given in a simple and easy-to-follow format.

The takeaway from Chanakya's mighty work is this: even if you are a pundit in your profession, never try to impress anyone with your achievements. If someone requires your counsel, just share the essence of your life experience and knowledge in short, simple and practical advice.

1.2

I declare it
With a wish for people's welfare
A scientific understanding of its basics
Makes a person all-aware

Chanakya continues the introduction of his book *Chanakya Neeti* by declaring the purpose of writing it; he says that he has penned it down for the welfare of people. It is not for any selfish interest, not to make his work famous and not for any personal glory. He also adds that the narrative style he has used in *Chanakya Neeti* is scientific in nature. By this he means that the verses inside these pages are logical and systematic, not some cluttered thoughts jotted down without a care. The views presented here are structured. So when you read the book, you will find it easy to understand and implement what you read in your everyday life. This will help you lead a fruitful life.

What is your wish?

Every person has one wish at the least that he wants fulfilled at any cost. What is that one wish you crave for day and night? Is it just to eat, live, earn money and die like billions of others? Or do you wish to do something good, something that will help other people. As Chanakya says, those who work for the welfare of others have a higher purpose in life. Leading a selfish life is nothing great, everyone does that. But using one's mind and heart for the benefit of others is the mark of great men. If you want to be a leader, be willing to serve others. Then, like magic, God will grant you many opportunities to work for the welfare of the masses. Your life will become an inspiration and you will be a role model for others.

Is your wish logical?

Never do anything without logic or a scientific approach. Science is not just a subject you learn in school; it is a way of methodical thinking. So before you do anything, you need to ask yourself—is my wish beneficial or harmful? What will the ideal outcome be? What will happen if things go wrong? What's my plan B? Prepare for both good and bad results. Once you cultivate a scientific bent of mind, you will approach everything rationally; you will be able to keep your head above our heart.

However, this does not mean one should not have emotions; just do not let emotions influence one's decisions. For this, one has to develop emotional intelligence—the ability to use emotional information to guide thoughts and behaviour, and manage emotions to achieve one's goal.

An emotionally intelligent person is able to respect his feelings as well as those of others, and not get carried away by them. It's good to remember the saying: have emotions but do not become emotional.

Are you aware of everything?

One should not lead one's life in darkness. Darkness is not just about the absence of light in the physical sense; the real darkness is ignorance—about the world and oneself. So at the worldly level, one should be well read and well informed. Chanakya wants us to be worldly wise so that others won't be able to fool us. Being mindful will give us the strength to deal with difficult people and circumstances.

Also, one should be aware of the self. If you notice, your mind is seldom under your control. You struggle to understand your own feelings and emotions. As one is aware of the outside world, one should also have the understanding of the inner world—the world of thoughts, feelings and emotions. This is called self-awareness.

1.3

By studying this scripture,
A person learns the truth of the matter
About celebrated teachings in those scriptures,
Dos and don'ts, beneficial and sinister

Chanakya explains what happens when a person studies *Chanakya Neeti*. He will understand the real truth of the matter, the reality of life. Also, he will be exposed to the thoughts of great people who wrote other scriptures, because he had read many of them to compile his own, to help the common man. If you do not understand these writings, you will miss out on many good lessons within these verses.

Scriptures or holy texts like the Vedas, *shastras*, *puranas*, etc., are also codes of conduct. They teach you what is right and what is wrong, what to do and not to do, how to behave and how not to behave. These are important cues for living harmoniously with other people. Study of scriptures will give you insights about the world, so you will be prepared to face any eventualities and even to escape them, if need be. Chanakya takes these valuable teachings and condenses them in one single book, *Chanakya Neeti*.

Study the scriptures

It is important to read holy texts on a daily basis. It should be a part of your routine, like waking up or brushing your teeth. Reading sacred literature is a daily mental, intellectual and spiritual exercise. It should be done in the mornings, before you face the world. It will make you strong from within; you will be able to face any challenge from a spiritual angle. A person who reads the scriptures daily over a period of time will transform into a spiritual individual—someone who is devoid of vices like anger, greed, envy, etc.

Know about great thoughts

Holy texts are open secrets. But you need to open their pages to know the surprises contained in them. There are secrets of this world and the other world inside them. It will only take you one little step to open these great writings and read them, and with a bit of effort, you will be introduced to a new world of thoughts and ideas. These scriptures are written by great men and women. They were no ordinary people. They were intellectual and spiritual dynamos. And these people had great point of views. When you start reading these scriptures (*shastras*), these thoughts permeate your mind as well. You will realise that you are suddenly exposed to a new world of amazing possibilities.

What to do and not to do

These *shastras* also contain rules. They provide a code of conduct, customs, dos and don'ts to follow in day-to-day life. Our forefathers, the great rishis who wrote the scriptures, realised that the common man required guidance to understand certain subtle aspects of life. So to make it easy for commoners to go through life, they thought it best to lay down certain social codes in the form of prayers, rituals, hymns, etc.

These sacred writings also provide suggestions to become successful in worldly matters too. They gave instructions on how to run a business, how to handle enmity, how to manage wealth, how to raise a family, etc. They also have information on certain laws and penalties from a legal standpoint as well.

The essence of the scriptures is to help one lead a successful and spiritual life. And finally find total happiness—in this world and the one beyond.

CHAPTER 2

SPIRITUAL WISDOM

2.1

The *Vipra* is like a tree, whose roots are prayers
The Vedas are his branches; his deeds are the leaves
Therefore, diligently keep the roots secure
Cutting off the roots, neither the branches
Nor the leaves endure

Mahatma Gandhi said, "A man is but the product of his thoughts. What he thinks, he becomes." If you nurture a mind that is always complaining, you will still feel miserable in the most comfortable situations in life. The secret to living a content life is understanding that comforts and luxury do not bring happiness. It is your mindset and quality of thoughts that determine your quality of life. So always maintain a prayerful attitude towards life. Those people who are grateful for what they have, experience peace and happiness throughout their lives.

In the above *neeti*, Chanakya says that one should carry on in life with a prayerful disposition. Here he gives the example of a wise man (*Vipra* in Sanskrit) and compares him to a tree.

A wise man's prayers are his roots

The roots of a tree are its very foundation; the deeper the roots, the stronger the tree. In the same manner, Chanakya advises us to live a prayerful life. You can't see the roots of a tree because they exist below the surface of the earth. But it is through the roots that the whole tree is nourished. In the same way, always be devout. You prayers don't have to be showcased for the outside world. But a prayerful outlook will mentally strengthen you.

The Vedas are the branches

Branches are the veins of the tree; they carry nutrients up from the roots. According to Chanakya, the Vedas are the branches. The Vedas are supposed to be *apaurushiya*, meaning not created by human beings. They contain the eternal wisdom of the universe. This wisdom was revealed to some great *rishis* in the past. And they documented this wisdom in the form of four holy books—*Rig Veda, Yajur Veda, Sama Veda* and *Atharva Veda*. A man who studies the Vedas, and after grasping its essence, shares this wisdom with others for their benefit is certainly wise.

His deeds are the leaves of the tree

Leaves prepare food for the tree. An idle person will not enjoy a fulfilling life, just as a tree without leaves won't thrive. Same is the case with great men; they need to fulfill their responsibilities to keep them going. It is a myth that wise men just sit and meditate all day and don't contribute anything to the world. All wise men continue to carry out their obligations. It is the calling of the wise to serve others. In that sense, a self-realised person works much more than all of us put together. So if you want to achieve self-realisation, service is the way forward. Great men and women live by this principle. And what do fruits of a tree represent? They represent happiness. By serving others unconditionally, one achieves happiness. But all this is dependent on the roots. No tree can exist without roots. Therefore, keeping a prayerful attitude, dedicate your life to the service of others.

2.2

What worry is there in my life
If Hari is the world's sustainer
Were He not so, how for the child's sustenance
Could the milk flow from the breasts of the mother?
Thinking so again and again
O Lord of the Yadus and Lord of Lakshmi,
Serving only your lotus feet ever and always
Time passes for me

In this verse, you get to see Chanakya's *bhakti*. Chanakya is known for his brilliant political ideas and shrewd stratagems. But here we find the same Chanakya professing his love for Lord Vishnu (Hari), who is the husband of goddess Lakshmi.

Where there is faith, there is no worry. So Chanakya asserts that when Lord Vishnu is the sustainer and provider of the whole universe, there's no need for him to worry. He continues his praise with an example of mother and child.

Mother and child

Nature is a perfect provider; nature has everything we require. Our problem is that we ask for more than what we need and when we don't get it, we get upset. Chanakya says that even a newborn is cared for by the Lord Almighty. As soon as a child is born, nature provides milk in the breasts of the mother; breast milk is wholesome food for a child. A newborn doesn't require any other nourishment for his survival other than his mother's milk.

Developing devotion

When you think of such examples, you realise that everything is created and maintained by God. Why should then you ever worry?

God knows what is best for you. It is said, "You do not get what you desire but what you deserve." Such thinking always helps to develop devotion within us. And when devotion develops in you, you automatically turn to service. Through service of the Lord, you serve people around you, and this will make you truly happy.

Passing time

When one is devoted to God, one is never stressed; not worried about what is going to happen. Time passes without one's notice. This way, one is able to live life contended and happy. There are no more desires or anxieties. One is able to take life as it comes; go with the flow. And whatever comes, one is able to view it as a Godsend opportunity to serve others. Chanakya himself lived such a devoted and noble life.

2.3

**Without oblations to the scared fire,
the Vedas are chanted in vain
So are religious ceremonies without donation
Without faith nothing is accomplished
Therefore, faith is indeed the causation**

Faith can move mountains. Chanakya takes two examples of interdependency to establish this point. One is paying obeisance to the sacred fire. And the other is religious ceremonies. Chanakya uses both these examples to talk about faith and its power.

Paying oblations to the sacred fire

In Vedic culture, there are various rituals involving the lighting of the sacred fire. Priests offer ghee, coconut, sandal wood, etc., to the fire while chanting mantras. According to Chanakya, without such offerings as prescribed in the Vedas, a *yajna* is not complete.

Religious ceremonies and donations

During religious ceremonies, after completing all the rituals, the one hosting the ceremony has to offer donations (*dakshina*) to the priests who conducted the ceremony, to the elders and gurus who were present during the ceremony and seek their blessings. One can give these donations as per one's capacity and wish. But without this act of giving *dakshina*, no ceremony is complete.

Faith and a person's life

In the same way, a person's life is not complete without faith. Faith is different from hope; it is the complete trust in someone or something (not necessarily religious in nature). It is a noble quality that will help you to move forward in life. Faith provides the spiritual strength to face problems. Without faith nothing can be accomplished but with faith one can achieve the impossible. So here Chanakya is trying to point out that life is intertwined with faith. If you don't have faith, you have nothing to motivate you, to propel you towards great heights. To be alive and active, you need faith in yourself, your mentors and God.

2.4

For a *Dvija*, God is in the fire
For a sage, God is in his heart
God is in the idol for the dim-witted
But everywhere for the just

What you see and how you perceive what you see define your personality. Different people could see the same thing and still perceive it differently. For example, a child looks at a smartphone as a toy but for an adult the same smartphone represents a microcosm of the whole world, what with the work emails, social networks, entertainment apps, online finance platforms, so on and so forth. So is the case with God. God represents different things to different people. Chanakya is giving an example using four types of people who see God differently.

Seeing God in the fire

Dvija in Sanskrit means twice-born, like a bird—a mother bird lays an egg first and then the hatchling emerges from the egg. So people who have gone through the process of spiritual initiation (through rituals like the thread ceremony in the case of Brahmins) are also called Dvija—those who are first born from the mother's womb and then attains a second birth as a spiritual person. For such a person who is initiated into daily rituals, he sees God in the sacred fire while he does his daily pooja and in the yajnas he participates in.

God in the heart

For a sage, God is always in his heart. A sage's heart is filled with devotion and is only focused on God. He does not look at the outside world to find God. He searches for God inside himself.

God in idols

Many of us indulge in idol worship. According to Chanakya, such people limit themselves only to the form of God as represented by the idol. They keep fighting over one form of God or the other. Therefore, he calls such people dim-witted.

God is everywhere

Wise are those who see God everywhere and in everything. One who realises that God is omnipresent is really an accomplished person. He is just and noble. And such a person is always clear-headed. If you develop this mindset, you will be able to achieve the highest state of happiness on earth.

2.6

No austerity measures up to calmness No joy is better than contentment No disease is worse than greed And no religion cuts above compassion

Here Chanakya talks about calmness, contentment, greed and compassion, and through them shows us how to be good human beings.

Austerity and joy

Being austere is great. Leading a simple life without excesses has its merits. The less materialistic you are, the more you will cherish other aspects of life: the warmth of human relationships, goodness of nature, etc. However, no austerity measures up to the ability to remain calm under all circumstances. Life can be full of challenges, day in and day out. But if a person can keep his cool and get through his trials, he is already a winner.

In the same way, no joy can match the feeling of contentment—the feeling of satisfaction drawn from one's circumstances; being at ease with one's life. This is a more fixed form of happiness than momentary joy or elation. No external factors can bring that kind of happiness to a person. It has to come from within. A content man is the happiest in the world.

Disease and religion

The worst disease a man can catch is greed. Greed makes a person so unsatisfied that he is bound to lose his peace of mind. Greed will never be satiated and a greedy person will never experience contentment, the greatest joy on earth.

And finally, the greatest religion is compassion—kindness towards other fellow beings. No matter what religion he belongs to, a man who has no empathy for another's plight will never find God. God is not in any idol or in any prayer hall; He is in each of us, so treat each other with compassion because when you treat another man right, you are worshipping God. When you appreciate the importance of these four qualities discussed, you will become a better, wholesome individual.

2.7

Kalpavriksh is just a tree;
Sumeru is a mountain; Chintamani is just a stone;
The sun's rays are hot; the moon wanes;
And the ocean's water is salty;
Kamadeva is without a body; Bali is a king of demons;
Kamadhenu is just a beast;
None of these can be compared to you, O Raghupate!

Even the best of people have some flaw or the other; nothing is faultless or blemish-free. Chanakya lists several splendid people and objects in mythology. But looking at their imperfections, his conclusion is that one can find defects in everything. But it is only Raghupati, Lord Rama, who is perfect, without comparison.

Kalpavriksh, Sumeru, Chintamani, the sun and the moon

The mythological wish-granting tree called Kalpavriksh may be great, but finally it is just a tree. The greatest mountain, Sumeru (also called Mount Kailas), cannot move. Chintamani, the wish-granting stone, is only a rock. The sun may provide warmth and sustain life but sunrays are scorching hot and one cannot stand the heat beyond a point. And the moon is beautiful but wanes with time.

The ocean, Kamadeva, Bali and Kamadhenu

The ocean is mighty and vast, but what is the point when it is so salty that its water cannot be consumed? Kamadeva, who is the god of love, does not even have a physical form. Bali, the great generous king, is a descendant of demons. And Kamadhenu, the divine cow, is still an animal even though it resides in heaven. All these powerful things and beings are still faulty when we take a close look at them. Therefore, Chanakya says, the only thing that is flawless is Raghupati, God himself.

2.8

**The deity dwells not in a piece of wood,
In a stone or in a clay model
In faith surely is He, therefore, it is faith
In the deity that is fundamental**

What exactly is faith? And where can you find it? A lot of confusion exists among people regarding the understanding of faith. Does God exist in idols made of wood, stone and clay? Or is He somewhere else? Chanakya is able to provide an answer here for this timeless question.

God is not in wood, stone or clay idols

The images of God we find around are made of various materials like wood, stone or clay. But those idols are only representations of

God. God doesn't dwell in those man-made idols. It is when you add your faith to those figurines the real God awakens. You must have heard stories of people who couldn't visit temples or other places of worship owing to their disabilities, difficult circumstances, etc., but were still able to experience the presence of God. These devotees were able to feel the divine presence because of their unshakable faith in Him.

God is in your faith

Without faith, any statue of God is just a piece of wood or stone or clay. The essence of God is in the faith of his devotee. *Shraddha* is the fundamental power in a person. Where there is faith, there is surrender to God. And in that total acceptance, God reveals Himself to us.

2.9

Desires of the mind!
Who has got all cushy things?
Everything depends on destiny
Therefore, count your blessings!

The mind is very tricky; just when you have fulfilled one desire, it comes up with another. You may have everything you want, and yet a new desire will always crop up. So all the comfortable things you already possess cannot guarantee you true happiness.

Your destiny

According to Chanakya, everything you have is yours because of your destiny. What is destined for you will surely come to you unasked. Destiny and your luck play a major role in your life, whether you are aware of it or not. So do work hard towards your desires and ambition. However, you will only get what you are destined to receive.

Count your blessings

Instead of building upon the desires of the mind, which are never-ending, you should count your blessings. When you do that, you will happily realise that you are blessed with many things other, less-fortunate people wish for. So be happy and contended with what you have. Leave the rest to your destiny.

2.10

Egoism gets dissolved
In the knowledge of the Supreme Soul
Then wherever the mind goes
There it meets the Ultimate Goal

This verse describes the state of an enlightened person. His egoism has ended. It has dissolved. The person is free from the clutches of his mind and problems that comes with a strong ego. How did such a person reach the egoless state? Chanakya explains how using this verse.

Knowledge of the Supreme Soul

The Supreme Soul, the ultimate knowledge called *atma vidya*, has awakened in an enlightened person. His ego has vanished with this ultimate knowledge, the realisation of God. And the person is free and not dependent on anything else for his happiness. He is content with himself.

One's state of mind

How does such a person think? An enlightened person's mind also functions just like any other mind. But his thoughts are different. Wherever such a mind goes, it's able to see God. God is everywhere and in everything for such a person. This is the state of true self-realisation.

Most complications in a person's life arise from that individual's ego. So shed your ego and see how uncomplicated life becomes then. In order to enjoy the happiness of being in the moment—which is what matters the most—one needs to have an ego-free mind.

2.11

**The human mind is indeed
The cause of bondage and deliverance
The love of pleasure enslaves
But detachment liberates**

There is a famous saying—'Your mind is your greatest friend and your worst enemy.' Chanakya highlights the same idea in the above verse. The same mind that binds you down can also set you free; it depends on how you use it.

The love of pleasure enslaves

We are constantly running behind desires. We want to be happy; we also want to avoid any kind of unhappiness and misery. Our mind is either constantly on a quest to find happiness or trying to run away from unhappiness. When one goes in search of pleasure, one becomes a slave to one's own mind and its cravings.

Detachment liberates

Chanakya says that if you manage to stay detached from your

material possessions and relationships, you will be free. This state of indifference will liberate you. In Sanskrit, this detachment is called *vairagya*. One can achieve this state by practicing meditation. Start by watching your thoughts drift by without pursuing them. This will slowly help you see the world in a different light; from a third-person's point of view and not from a participant's. Learn to control your mind. Don't be a slave to your thoughts. Instead, master your mind and make it work for your benefit.

2.12

Nothing more than passion causes distraction
There is no bigger enemy than delusions of the mind
Nothing burns more than anger
No bigger happiness than an enlightened mind

Your inner qualities can make or break you. There are positive qualities like love, faith, kindness, etc., that can lift you to a higher level of existence. But there are also many innate negative qualities that can destroy you if you are not careful with them. Chanakya in this verse is pointing out a few negative qualities that need to be weeded out for a person to be happy.

Passion, delusion and anger will harm you

When the mind is zealous, it is difficult to concentrate. And this causes the work at hand to suffer. It is easy to get lost in the delusions of the mind. Chanakya also cautions that nothing burns more than anger. Anger is the root cause of all problems. It is good to remember Lord Buddha's words here: "Holding on to anger is like grasping a hot coal with the intent of throwing it at someone else; you are the one who gets burned."

Enlightenment is true happiness

Where do you find happiness? True, lasting joy? It is always inside you. The process of finding your inner happiness is a spiritual journey. At the end of that journey, you will be more aware of who you are and what makes you happy. All the great sages, thinkers and philosophers finally came to the conclusion that only enlightened minds are able to experience ultimate happiness. So aim for a mind that is free of pettiness and competition.

2.13

Anger is the regent of death
Greed is the river of hell
Knowledge is the wish-granting cow
Contentment is the celestial garden

Once again Chanakya advises us to avoid anger and greed. And he also urges mankind to follow the pursuit of knowledge and not to be materialistic. The wise teacher Chanakya wanted his students to be perfect inside as well as outside. He believed that if you conquer the mind, you will be able to conquer the world.

Anger and greed

Anger is the regent of death. So if Yama, the lord of death, wants to take a soul from earth, all he has to do is provoke him. A person who constantly gets angry will slowly succumb to death because his body and mind will suffer from the burning anger within, leading to many diseases. And Chanakya compares greed to the river from hell. A river flows with no restraint, with tricky undercurrents; greed is just like a river in that sense, flowing unchecked, with danger lurking just beneath. In order to satiate his avarice, a greedy person will slowly move towards immoral paths that will lead him to a world full of trouble.

Knowledge and contentment

If one wants to acquire anything, one should pursue knowledge. Knowledge is wealth; a person with a degree is more likely to land a job, a high-paying one that too, than an illiterate person. A learned man can make his own way in the world using his acumen. So if a man wants to get wealthy, acquiring wisdom is the best way forward. Wealth always follows the wise, like a wish-granting cow (*Kamadhenu*). And finally, a person should be contented with what he has. The state of mind of a contented person is like being in the celestial garden; everything is so rich and beautiful there. However, the real beauty lies in a calm and composed mind. If you have such a psyche then you can experience heavenly bliss right here on earth.

2.14

Having read the four Vedas
And several scriptures
Yet living without realising the soul
Is like the sweetness of food unknown to the ladle

You must read to acquire knowledge. But what use is knowledge if it has not been digested? There are many bookworms who read non-stop. But if you look at their lives, many of them show no signs of intelligence. Just gathering information is not enough. You should be able to apply that information in daily life to reap its benefits.

Acquiring knowledge

There are many scholars who have by-hearted all the Vedas — the *Rig Veda*, *Sama Veda*, *Yajur Veda* and *Atharva Veda*. They would have also read many other scriptures like the *puranas*, the *Ramayana*, the *Mahabharata*, the *Upanishads* and others. Chanakya holds these

learned people in high regard only if they are able to implement
the teachings in theses texts their daily life.

Know your soul

Chanakya says that only reading the scriptures without understanding
one's own soul is like using the ladle that serves food. The ladle
scoops food every time it is used to serve the dish, but has no idea
how delicious or rich the preparation is. This is just like a person
who gorges on books but learns little from the pages full of wisdom.
Therefore, read in order to realise the truth of your own soul.

2.15

**As fragrance in a flower, oil in sesame seed,
Fire in wood, butter in milk,
And sweetness in sugarcane
One should seek the soul in a body**

In the above verse, Chanakya talks about the importance of having
a soul. A body without a soul is like a flower without fragrance.

The real essence

A flower's richness is in its fragrance. We search for oil in sesame
seeds. Wood is useful only when it can light a fire; wet wood is of
no use to anyone. When we churn milk, we get butter. Sugarcane
carries sugar in its fibers. Just as we search for the essence in these
things, we should look for the soul in the body.

The importance of soul

The body is just the outer covering of a person. To know a person
well, instead of focusing on outer beauty and other worldly
accomplishments, search for the soul in a person, his real essence —

who he really is; the core of his personality. There is a famous quote floating around on the internet that says, "You don't have a soul; you are a soul. You have a body." Many religions believe that even after the death of a person, the soul continues to exist. Only the mortal body perishes, the soul is immortal.

2.16

Look before you take a step
Filter the water through a cloth before you sip
Conform to the scriptures while speaking up
For conscience's sake, obey its whip!

Chanakya's instructions about the right conduct for daily practice are given in this verse. People mostly get in trouble because of their thoughtless behaviour. Make sure to follow the master's advice for a less chaotic life.

Better safe than sorry

If you walk on the streets with your eyes closed, you're sure to fall into a ditch or be run over by a vehicle. Likewise, drinking unfiltered water can also be harmful. Before electric water filters, people used clean cloth as a sieve to filter drinking water. Chanakya uses these examples to show us to be careful in life.

Conform to the scriptures, listen to your conscience

The scriptures or *shastras* are guidebooks; they share advice on what to do and what to avoid. Life has a tendency to throw googlies when you least expect them. So when you are in doubt regarding what to say, don't say anything impulsively. Chanakya advises us to consult the scriptures before speaking up. Also, when you are in a dilemma, just listen to your conscience. What people usually call "gut feeling" is often their inner wisdom speaking to them. Even if what your conscience tells you to do is like a whip that hurts, obey it. Be assured that your decision will be the right one.

2.17
Everyone experiences birth and death alone
Everyone stands up to good and bad actions alone
Everyone faces hell alone
Everyone reaches heaven alone

We come to this earth alone and we leave it alone. Others are just a part of our life journey. However, there is a big difference between being alone and being lonely. Most of us feel lonely when we don't have people around us. But once we understand that we are always alone, we will enjoy being alone and also the company of others, in a more detached manner.

Everyone is alone

We are born alone. And we also die alone. Life is always the journey of an individual. All the experiences are ours to go through. Even if there are many people going through the same event, their experiences will be different. Also, when we have to face the consequence of our actions, be it good or bad, we have to face them alone.

Enjoy your own company

According to popular scriptures, after death come the experiences of heaven or hell. As in death, a person is alone in his journey of heaven or hell, depending upon his deeds on earth. According to most holy texts, if you have been good, you go to heaven, but if you have done bad things on earth, you will go to hell to suffer the consequences. However, all these experiences are yours alone. Nobody—be it your family, friends or others who love you—will be there with you to share it. Even if you don't believe in the concepts of heaven and hell, the facts that you were born alone and you will die alone don't change. So learn to enjoy your own company. After all, you are all you've got, in its truest sense.

2.18

Wealth, friends, spouse and land
One can obtain again
But this life as a human
Can't be had now and again

To be born a human being is a rare privilege indeed. Chanakya reminds us through this poignant verse that one can regain anything that one has lost, but not life as a human being. Remember this and make full use of the time you have.

Second chances

People always live in fear of losing what they possess; it could be wealth, friends, a spouse or land. Your hard-earned money can be stolen. You may lose a dear friend to a fight or death. Your loving spouse may leave you, and also the land that you own can be lost. But do not worry, because you can have all of them again; you can acquire more wealth, you can find new friends, marry another person or buy a new plot of land. All of these can be recovered.

Life as a human

There is no guarantee that you will be born again. Life is a rare gift. Only if you are alive will you be able to earn all that is lost back. Better make good use of your life now. Spend your life serving others and through good deeds strive to attain liberation when it's time for you to leave your mortal body.

2.19

Poverty, sickness, suffering, Bondage and addiction By the tree of self-repression Is caused their fruition

When it comes to poverty, sickness, suffering, bondage and addiction, it's human tendency to blame others. But Chanakya says that they are all results of self-repression, the result of keeping one's thoughts and feelings concealed for ages.

Poverty, sickness, suffering, bondage and addiction

Have you ever heard of somebody wanting to be poor forever? Or that someone is happy being sick? No one likes suffering (physical or psychological). Neither do people like to be oppressed or imprisoned. Addiction to something (narcotics, alcohol, fast-food, people…) can ruin lives.

Self-repression is a tree that bears bad fruits

According to Chanakya, all suffering arises from self-repression. He compares it to a tree that bears bad quality fruits. When one's thoughts, wishes and feelings are kept under wraps, they erupt in other forms, like diseases, addiction, etc. It is best to express yourself, in any form possible. Find an outlet for your feelings and you will feel much better. You may even find inspiration to be more creative or do some good deeds in the process.

2.20

Where Lakshmi is the mother
Vishnu is the father
Devotees of Vishnu are kinsfolk
The motherland itself represents the triple sphere

A family is a unit consisting of many individuals. But the most important members are the mother, father and children. In India, family is given the utmost importance and we are always told that blood is thicker than water. Chanakya in this particular verse is describing the importance of having an ideal family in one's life.

The bond between family members

Here Chanakya compares the mother of the family to Goddess Lakshmi—the goddess of wealth and prosperity. It's the presence of a good mother that turns a house into a home; she nourishes and provides for everyone. The father is compared to Lord Vishnu— the one who sustains the family with his love and by maintaining discipline. Chanakya says that the children of a family should be like ardent devotees who follow the advice of their father and mother.

Motherland and triple sphere

Chanakya says that the three worlds—heaven, earth and hell— become home to the one who has Lakshmi as his mother, Vishnu as his father and worshippers of Vishnu as his relatives.

To further highlight the importance of family, here's the story of Ganesha and Kartikeya, the sons of Lord Shiva and goddess Parvathi. Once the brothers had a competition to establish who among them was the fastest. They decided to race around the world. It was decided that whoever returns to the starting point first will be the winner. Kartikeya at once sat on his peacock and went off. But Ganesha, using his wisdom, simply circumambulated his parents. When his brother returned, Ganesha told him that his world is his parents and so he had finished the task much earlier. This story highlights the importance of family and the respect and love one should have for one's parents.

2.21

In the midst of thousands of cows
A calf pursues its mother
Past actions follow the doer
In a similar way

According to Hinduism and Buddhism, karma is the force generated by a person's actions (either in this life or in the past life) that dictates the state of events in his present life. Karma is considered the universal law of cause and effect. In this verse, Chanakya explains the connection between one's actions and their consequences.

Karma is like a calf who seeks its mother

In the midst of a herd of cows, a calf always knows who its mother is and will only pursue its mother for milk. No one else will do. Similarly, our actions—whether good or bad—belong to us and follow us. No one can escape the consequences of one's actions by blaming others. As you sow, so shall you reap.

Actions of the past follow you

The law of karma doesn't spare anyone. All actions have consequences. Be it good or bad. These consequences will reach you unasked. You get what you deserve; no one can escape karma. What you have sown will bare its fruits sooner or later.

2.22

If leaves don't grow on a karira tree
Is the spring season to blame?
If the owl can't see during the day
Is it the fault of the sun?
If raindrops fall not into the mouth of the cuckoo
Is it the cloud's mistake?
Who has the power
To wipe off the destiny inscribed on one's forehead?

This is a beautiful and powerful verse. A man's destiny cannot be changed. Even if you put in your best effort, you will get only what's destined for you. Chanakya gives a few examples to stress the role of destiny in this world.

Karira tree, owl and raindrops

Karira is a type of tree that grows in arid climates and does not have any leaves. It's not the fault of the spring season that the karira doesn't bear leaves. It's in the make-up of the tree itself. Likewise, an owl cannot see in daylight. But it's not the fault of the sun. An owl is programmed to function normally in the dark of the night. Again, if the cuckoo bird cannot get raindrops directly into its mouth as soon as it rains, the cloud isn't to be blamed. The cuckoo can very well drink the water collected on the ground.

Destiny written on one's forehead

It is said that a man's destiny is written on his forehead, and what is written there cannot be erased. So who is to blame for one's misfortune? No one. Because no one has the power to change a person's destiny; it is said that people are born with their fate already decided by the celestial powers. If at all there is anyone who can alter your destiny, it is you alone. So don't be disheartened by failures and struggles. If victory is in your cards, no one will be able to take it away from you.

2.23

Life span, occupation, wealth, Education and how one's death will occur These five are determined while a person Is in the womb of his mother

According to Chanakya, even before a person is born his fate has been decided by the celestial powers. Through this verse, he asserts that a person's life is largely pre-decided.

Life span, occupation and wealth

Even the healthiest person has to die one day. Scriptures say that the longest a human being can live is 120 "smiling" years. Chanakya says, as in the case of a person's lifespan, his profession and wealth are also written in his stars.

Education and death too

What kind of education a person receives and how this person is going to die are also pre-decided, says Chanakya. According to Chanakya, all this is determined when a human being is in his mother's womb. So make the best out of the time you are given on this earth without getting bogged down by life. Try to live each day as if it is your last and you will find a new appreciation for time.

2.24

Time matures all beings
Time annihilates people
Time stays awake when everybody is asleep
Time is indeed unbeatable

Time, what a mystery it is! Time is like a magic wand that can turnaround anything in a split of a second—a king into a pauper and a pauper into an Emperor. Those who really understand time surrender to it. Wise men know that nothing can stop time.

Time matures people

Experience and maturity come with time. A child evolves as he becomes an adult because of his life experiences. Time can even dethrone conquerors. It can annihilate people when they least expect it.

Time is always awake

We sleep but time does not. The clock is always ticking. Time is the only thing a man cannot overcome. It is indeed unbeatable, all powerful and all decisive. Use your time wisely and respectfully. Know that with time things change; it is inevitable—good or bad. Be prepared to face the best and the worst. It's probably for the best that nothing lasts forever.

2.25

As is the desire of Providence
So functions one's intellect
One's activities are also controlled by Providence
And by the will of Providence one is surrounded by helpers

It is said that fate decides a man's course for him. Chanakya says our journeys are predestined; a person's destiny is controlled by Providence.

Providence and intellect

A person's intellect is controlled by Providence, says Chanakya. Which is probably the reason why when a person's luck goes south, his mind veers off the course as well, prompting him to make bad decisions, pick fights and attract further misfortune.

Fortune is a slave of Providence too

You must have heard many rags-to-riches stories; stories of ordinary people from humble backgrounds who hit a jackpot and became successful overnight. According to Chanakya, these changes in destinies are orchestrated by Providence. Heavenly wisdom is infinite and unfathomable to the human mind. Therefore, always be gracious and thankful to God in success. Who knows when a person's fate is going to change!

2.26

The lowbrow becomes king
The king is made miserly
The rich become poor
The poor are made rich by destiny

Who can stop fate and time? When the right time arrives, one's destiny shifts. Chanakya was a person who believed in planning and hard work. However, he knew that there are various things that are beyond human efforts and understanding. What you get is your destiny, how you get it is through hard work.

A lowly person can also become king one day

Even a person from the lowest section of society with no opportunities can become a king when luck blesses him. There are many millionaires and even billionaires in the world who made their fortunes overnight. On the contrary, the most powerful king can lose everything, become miserable and miserly when his fortune reverses.

The rich can become poor in no time

Just as the rich can lose all their wealth, the poor can suddenly become rich. Therefore, Chanakya is sharing an eternal truth that power and wealth are both linked to destiny. If you are powerful, it's because of your destiny. If you are rich, it's again because of your destiny. Thank your stars and remain humble because you never know when the tide will turn.

2.27

**No one has built a golden deer
No one has seen or heard of one
Yet Raghunandan was fascinated by it
At the time of destruction, one's mind works perversely**

Sometimes logic fails even gods. When misfortune sneaks up on you, you will forget to apply your intelligence. And in an altered state of mind, it is easy to take decisions that will cost you dearly. Here in the above verse Chanakya uses a famous example from the *Ramayana* to drive home his point.

The golden deer that never existed

In one of the pivotal events in the *Ramayana*, Mareech, an accomplice of the demon king Ravana, disguises himself as a golden deer to entice Sita. Sita falls for the golden deer and wants it at any cost. When her husband Rama and brother-in-law Lakshmana go after the deer, Sita is left alone in their hut in the forest. As a result, Ravana is able to kidnap her, an event that led to a bloody war between Rama and Ravana. However, the golden deer was just an illusion, it never existed. Not only did Sita fall into the trap but Lord Rama himself believed it and had to endure the misfortune of losing his wife as well as a result.

Adversities and reason

Logic and reason desert a person when his luck runs out. Even gods and men who are supposed to be *avatar purush* were not spared adversities. What does that say about mere mortals like us? Pay attention to all the minute details while making a decision. Don't underestimate anyone or anything because luck is fickle and can turn one's life upside down in a moment.

2.28

Truth supports the earth
Truth kindles the sun
Truth blows the wind
Truth sustains everyone

Our culture gives top most priority to truth. Chanakya himself was a seeker of truth who realised the importance of sharing his wisdom with the rest of the world.

Truth supports the earth, the sun and the wind

According to Chanakya, the earth is supported by the power of truth. It is the power of truth that makes the sun shine and winds blow. The very life on this universe is sustained by truth and truth alone.

Truth sustains everyone

All things rest upon truth. Only when there is truth, there is trust. And without trust, the universe will crumble like an eggshell trodden by an elephant.

The power of truth in the words of Dalai Lama: "Try to remain truthful. The power of truth never declines. Force and violence may be effective in the short term, but in the long run, it's truth that prevails."

2.29

**The spirit sets itself in motion
By itself enjoys the gains
By itself roams about the world
And from there attains liberation**

The soul gets caught in the circle of karma and gets out of it on its own. Nobody on earth can escape the snares of karma. Life is the journey of the soul; it goes through the good and bad consequences of its actions and finally gets liberated at the end of the karmic cycle.

The soul goes through its own karma

As we go through life, we accrue the good and bad results of our actions. Our souls go through these encounters on their own and no soul can truly share its journey with another; it's a solitary experience.

The soul frees itself

No matter what, everyone has to go through life on their own account. The soul of a person gets caught in the cycle of birth and death and all the drama that comes with it. The soul goes through life trying to get out of this circle. Finally, when the soul leaves the body of a person in the event of his death, it's liberated from that particular karmic cycle.

2.30

"Shame upon those who do not worship the lotus feet of
Shri Krishna, Mother Yashoda's son
Shame upon those who have no attachment to the
Tales describing the glories of Shrimati Radharani
Shame upon those whose ears are not eager to listen to
The stories of the Lord's *lila*,"
Exclaims the *mridanga* sound '*dhik-tam dhik-tam
dhigatam*' during *kirtana*

What is the meaning of life if a person does not develop love and
devotion to God? You can achieve everything in this world—name,
fame, success, beauty and wealth. But what use are they if you don't
have place for God in your heart? Chanakya gives a classic example
of Lord Krishna here to bring out the devotion within us.

The glory of worship

Chanakya says that those who do not worship the son of Yashoda,
that is Lord Krishna, or those who haven't heard the glories of his
beloved Radha, or who don't have the time to listen to the divine
play of Shri Krishna through *bhajans* and *kirtans* have not tasted
the nectar of devotion.

The sound of *mridanga*

During *kirtans* or *bhajans*, it's customary to play the Indian classical
instrument *mridanga* to add to the mood. According to Chanakya,
through the tune it plays, the *mridanga* is calling out to those in the
vicinity to come and join the worship.

2.31

A living person is as good as dead
If faithless
But even a dead person lives on
If he's devout

Continuing from the previous thought, Chanakya here once again points out the relevance of devotion. He glorifies devotees and praises them. About those who have not yet developed a spiritual lifestyle, he says that they are dead inside even though still alive physically.

An irreligious person is alive yet dead

Just because a person is breathing, walking around, doing chores doesn't mean that he's alive. According to Chanakya, those who do not worship God are not alive in the real sense; they are as good as dead. Only those who are pious are truly alive.

If you are devout, death is not the end of you

Those who are truly devoted to God never die. Their lives are so inspiring that even after the death of their mortal body they continue to live in the hearts of people. Just look around and you will see various temples, ashrams and spiritual places where saints and sages are remembered and worshipped even if they died a long time ago. They are worshipped eternally; they remain immortal through their devotion. If you are someone who is devoted to the Almighty, you will dedicate yourself to help others. Through these actions, others will love and cherish you even after you are long gone from the surface of the earth.

2.32

Descendants from heaven to this planet
Have four marks in their appearance:
Generosity, gentle voice,
Devotion to God and an attitude of service
towards Brahmins

Some people who take birth on earth are directly descended from
heaven, says Chanakya. They come down to earth to touch people's
lives. He guides us as to how to identify such people. He says they
have four special marks or qualities.

Generosity and a gentle voice

Such people are givers. They love to share everything they have.
They are great philanthropists; they are ready to share their wealth
with others. They are also very humble. They speak softly and
sweetly to others, never raising their voice. They treat others with
dignity. According to Chanakya, such people are God-incarnates
on earth and they manage to win the hearts of everyone around.

Devotion to God and respect for Brahmins

These noble souls are devotees of the lord and also serve everyone
around them. But most importantly, they serve Brahmins with their
whole heart. Brahmins are considered wise teachers who can impart
knowledge about various spiritual values and practices. Such great
men of learning are to be served. Chanakya says these are the four
qualities of people who have descendent from heaven. Seek out the
company of such people; you will get a chance to learn many good
things from them.

2.33

**Extreme anger, harsh speech,
Enmity with one's own relations, dishonesty,
Being friendly with unrefined people,
Service of the dishonourable
Are the marks of persons descended from hell**

As we saw the qualities of the people who have come down from heaven, Chanakya now elaborates on the quality of those who have come from hell.

Anger, harsh speech and enmity with one's own people

One prominent characteristic of those who have taken birth on this planet from hell is anger. To err is human and to get angry is natural. But too much wrath is not a good quality for a human being because we are social animals and an angry person with harsh speech is detrimental to any happy, peaceful environment. People get uncomfortable in such a person's presence. This could create a chasm between him and his relatives. Unlike those descended from heaven, such people do not share their wealth and are quite happy to see the misery of others.

Dishonesty, company of unrefined people and serving the dishnourable

One cannot trust those who never fulfill their promise and not even feel guilty about it. People who Chanakya say belong to hell like to team up and work with people of crude character. They enjoy bad company. And finally, they love to work with those with devious reputation. Stay away from such people; they only bring trouble.

2.34

Men have hunger, sleep, fear and copulation
In common with animals
But intelligence is something that differentiates
men from animals
Without intelligence a man is much the same
as an animal

What really differentiates human beings from animals? On the surface, both animals and humans eat, reproduce, live and die. But man is blessed with something very unique—intelligence. Man is considered God's superior creation because of his intellect.

Hunger, sleep, fear and copulation

Between an animal and man, four things are common: hunger, sleep, fear and copulation. These are our basic instincts. All living beings, in this case men and animals, feel hungry, need rest, experience fear and engage in copulation. These acts don't require thinking, they come naturally to us. When it comes to these basic instincts, men and animals are the same.

Intelligence separates men from animals

As human beings, we can ideate, innovate and create. According to science, human brain weighs more than that of all vertebrates relative to body size. Man is considered God's superior creation because of his intellect. Intelligence also has to do with the various components of the brain. The cerebral cortex in humans is highly developed as compared to other mammals, and this part is associated with memory, attention, perception, cognition, awareness, thought, language and consciousness. Because we are superior to animals in terms of intellect, we have to behave accordingly. If we do not

put our God-gifted intelligence to good use, what is the difference
between us and animals, asks Chanakya.

2.35

**Those who lack education, penance, knowledge,
Good disposition, virtue and benevolence
Are beasts wandering the surface of the earth
in the form of men
They are a burden to the earth**

Some people are only human in their physical appearance but
brutes by nature. Chanakya lists certain characteristics of such
people.

Lack of good qualities

People who are well-educated have a good disposition. They
know how to behave with others. They treat people with respect
and kindness. Wise souls believe in penance and are charitable.
And those people who lack learning, penance, knowledge, good
disposition, virtue and benevolence are wild animals roaming the
earth in human form. They are inferior to sensible men.

A burden to the earth

Vile people are no good to fellow beings. They only think of
themselves and won't lift a finger to help others. Instead they like
to create trouble for others and take delight in their misery. They
are not productive, neither are they a positive influence on others,
so Chanakya calls them a burden to the earth.

2.36

Even shackles can be strange
And the bond of love is the strongest
A bee, even though capable of perforating timber
Stays put within the petals of the lotus flower

In this verse Chanakya is trying to explain the invisible bonds that restrain us from reaching our potential with a simple example of a bee that lives in a lotus flower.

Chains of love

Shackles can be strange; they can be in any form, not necessarily metal chains. Even love can be used to tie up someone. And it's quite strong, mind you. "The root of suffering is attachment," says Buddha. Attachment also blocks self-realization. From love springs attachment and from attachment comes the fear of loss. As this fear grips a person, he is unable to unleash his full potential and conquer his goals. You fear the unknown because you get too comfortable where you are.

The bee and the lotus flower

A bee is capable of drilling through wood; it is quite a powerful little insect. But because it is infatuated with the lotus flower, it stays put within the petals of the lotus when petals close in the evening. This bee could have roamed about, exploring the world around him, but his love for the lotus confines him to that flower alone. Chanakya uses this metaphor to show how people waste opportunities that come their way due to certain attachments. Because of these invisible restraints don't be afraid to move out of your comfort zones; a whole new world awaits you outside with its infinite possibilities and experiences. Take a chance, try your luck. In the end you will only regret the things you didn't do.

2.37

Heaven-sent is the boat of *Dvija*
Which sails bottom-up in the ocean of life
Those who bow down to it skim through the water
While those hanging over it sink

A *Dvija* is a person who is twice-born. He is a person who has first
taken birth as a human being physically and then later is born again
spiritually, when he goes through the rites of passage and is initiated
into the world of Vedic wisdom. If such a person comes into your
life, it is because he is a godsend. Respect and serve all such saints,
sages and men of great wisdom.

The ocean of life

When you serve and listen to wise men, their words will help you
in crossing this turbulent ocean that is life. A wise man is like a boat
in the vast sea. He can help people who are stranded in the water
to reach the shore safely by imparting proper advice depending on
the seeker's situation. But strangely, Chanakya says the *Dvija's* boat
sails upside down. Here it implies that you need to surrender your
ego in the company of wise men to receive their help.

Sail across

Those who bow down to the *Divja*—those who listen to the wise
men and surrender to them—skim over the sea effortlessly. And
those who hang on to their egos sink in the ocean of *samsara*
(the cycle of death and rebirth), an endless circle of sorrows and
hardships. Sometimes in life, all you need is clarity of thought to
diffuse your nagging problems. It is possible for men of wisdom to
guide you and show you the light at the end of the tunnel, but only
if you want to. Only an egoless mind is able to seek help and grasp

new knowledge—an understanding of the ultimate truth that will help a man escape from the bondages of day-to-day life. Therefore, the only way to complete this journey of life is in the company of realised masters.

Do you have such mentors? Seeking help is not a sign of weakness but just the opposite. Don't let your ego stop you from reaching out and getting the best advice possible in any sticky situation you find yourself in.

2.38

**It is enough to live for a moment
If that moment is spent doing good deeds
It is useless living for ages and bringing only distress
To this world and the other**

Life is unpredictable. You could be alive one moment and dead the other. It is important to live a meaningful and a productive life till your last breath.

Do good deeds

If a person gets to live only for a second but that time is spent doing something good, like indulging in philanthropy or assisting someone in need, it is a life well lived. Life is precious. We are all intelligent human beings with infinite potential. So live every moment as it is the last and do be of help to others as much as possible.

Living for ages and bringing only distress

Better to live for a few moments doing good than to live for ages doing bad deeds. Even people who do small but significant work will be remembered for ages. Do you know the story about a tiny squirrel who helped Lord Ram? This squirrel assisted Ram and his monkey brigade to build a bridge across the sea to retrieve Sita from Lanka. According to Chanakya, living a meaningful but a short life is any day better than living for many years causing harm to others. People who only indulge in selfish activities are despised and uncared for by society. They are neither valued on earth nor in heaven.

2.39

**A true meal is the leftover of a Brahmin
True love is that which is shown to another
To abstain from sin is true wisdom
And true religion is the one which is practiced
without arrogance**

What exactly does being good mean? It means a life that is lived for others, only taking for oneself the bare minimum. Chanakya is advising us through this beautiful verse to live a fulfilling life through acts of compassion and sacrifice.

True food, true love and true wisdom

What kind of food is considered sacred or true? According to Chanakya, it is the leftover food from the meals of Brahmins, meaning wise people, saints and sages. It is also considered *prasad*. A good man eats only after offering food to others first, and such a meal is sacred. True love does not have expectations; true love only gives, unconditionally. And true wisdom knowing that one needs to keep away from crooked people and evil deeds.

True religion

According to Chanakya, a true, good religion is the one which is practiced without arrogance. Religious activities should be conducted with humility and the one who follows this dictum is truly faithful. Otherwise a religion becomes just a display of rituals and enlarges the follower's ego rather than eliminating it—the true purpose of any faith. And all world religions profess love and not hate towards fellow men, irrespective of their beliefs. So Chanakya urges people to be religious but not fanatical.

2.40

**Those who were not satiated with the enjoyment of wealth, food and women have all passed away
There are others now passing away who have likewise remained unsatiated
And in the future still others will pass away feeling themselves unsatiated**

Our whole life goes in amassing material comforts. And they become our objectives in life. We start appreciating valuables more than values. Chanakya, the excellent teacher that he was, gives us his view that everything we seek in life is finally going to be taken away from us. So why run behind physical comforts and material wealth at all?

Wealth, women and food

Here Chanakya is trying to explain the futility of worldly pleasures. We chase these three things continuously in our lives—wealth, women and food. We run after wealth—the poor trying to get rich, and the rich trying to get richer. It is a non-stop journey. Here Chanakya uses women as a symbol for physical attraction and lust. Men and women pursue each other and fall in love; it's been this way since the beginning of the human race. And food is also something we cannot do without. Many of us enjoy a good meal and often behave like we live for food alone.

Nothing is permanent

Even if you amass wealth, share pleasurable moments with the opposite sex and gobble up tasty food, all of this will end one day. Happiness from these activities is not permanent. We all have to leave this earth one day or the other. People will never have enough of all these pleasures. In the past many have died without having their thirst quenched. Many people die without fulfilling their desires. The same will happen in the future too. This is the true nature of life. Human desire is unappeasable.

2.41

The nectar of contentment fills joy
In peaceful people
It can't be had by the covetous
Restlessly running hither and thither

Contentment is the nectar that fills the heart with joy. People who are comfortable with what they have are always happy and peaceful. But people who are greedy and hold on to their possessions get destroyed by the very handle they are holding.

Joy of contentment

Many of us think that true happiness comes from fulfilling our wants. But that is not true. Because the moment we get what we want, the next one will rear its head. Yes, there is joy in achieving something, but that is only temporary. After a little while we will feel unhappy again and go in search of something new, something exciting. So a truly happy person is the one who is content with whatever he has in hand.

Covetous people

A greedy person will never experience joy in its truest form because he will never be content; he will always covet something and will run after it till he gets it. This cycle will continue till his death. Such is the miserable life of a covetous person. Don't fancy what others have. There will always be someone who is better than you in this world. Instead, concentrate on yourself. Try to appreciate everything you have, be it your family, career or possessions, and you will see how fortunate you are. There are many around the world who don't even have a roof to spend the night under or have a morsel to eat. How lucky you are compared to them!

2.42

**One who is attached stands in fear
Lovesickness is indeed a pot of sadness
For attachment is the cause of suffering
One gains happiness by being detached**

We get attached to many things in life, be it people or objects. And that is the biggest problem. If we are free from attachments, we can be truly happy.

Fear, lovesickness and suffering

Due to our attachment to our near and dear ones, we are subjected to the following—fear, lovesickness and suffering. As Chanakya explains, we suffer because we are tied to our family members and friends. We fear their loss, we fear the loss of their love; we seek intimacy and when we don't get what we expect, we feel sad.

Give up attachment

Fear of loss can prevent a person from being happy. Accept the realities of life—people die, things change and nobody can predict what is going to happen tomorrow. What's the point of worrying about the things that are not in your control? Once you accept this fact, you will be more at ease; you will be able to cherish every moment you spend with your loved ones.

2.43

**Listening to discourses one acquires righteousness
And is able to give up evil deeds
By listening one gains knowledge
And by listening one attains salvation**

Chanakya gives us a three-step process to gain happiness and attain salvation. They are: *shravan* (listening), *manan* (thinking) and *nidhidyasan* (meditation). Listen carefully and then think well about what one has heard. Finally, meditate on those thoughts. But the key question is, what to listen to?

Listen to spiritual discourses

According to Chanakya, listening to spiritual discourses given by great minds will help a person get rid of evil thoughts and attain a more ethical perspective. These discourses are called satsangs and many people today attend and benefit from such talks. Satsang in Sanskrit means "to be in the company of truth" or "in the company of good people". When one listens carefully to these spiritual gurus, one inevitably gains wisdom.

Salvation

Yes, by just listening to spiritual discourses over a long period of time, one can attain salvation, says Chanakya. We become what we listen to. And if we keep listening to something regularly and continuously, we develop the habit of thinking over what we have heard. And gradually we start to incorporate what we have heard into our lives. So listen to spiritual thoughts and slowly you will become spiritual in nature too.

2.44

**The frame of mind that comes about
During a discourse, sickness and cremation
If retained for good
Who will not gain salvation?**

In certain surroundings our minds tend to turn sober; profound thoughts crop up to guide us further. These thoughts could be very valuable and sacred. Chanakya names three such places where one could easily think of God and attain salvation in the process.

During spiritual discourses, sickness and cremation

It is but natural to think of God when one listens to spiritual discourses. It is the same with illness; people often think of God when they are unwell. No one likes to be sick and when we are not well we pray to heal quickly and get back on our feet. And who is not touched by the sight of a dead body? During the cremation of a family member or a close associate, most people contemplate life and its meaning, and about God's will.

Retain the feeling

Even though we think of God during the above mentioned situations, we do come out of our thoughts and go out in the world to lead our lives. We get busy and forget about our somber and spiritual thoughts. Chanakya says not to forget those spiritual musings; retain them and slowly they will lead us to *moksha*. Because when we think more about spiritual matters, we behave accordingly, and this paves the way for a better life in this world and the one beyond.

2.45

The poor want wealth
Animals want faculty of speech
Humans desire paradise
And the godly long for liberation

Everyone wants something. And our wants and desires keep us going in search of that "something".

Whether you are a man or animal, rich or poor, your desires are unlimited. In this *neeti*, Chanakya explains the never-ending list of wishes using interesting examples.

The poor and animals

The poor want wealth; they want to be rich. They need money for themselves and their family. For the poor, money is their first and basic desire. Animals wish for the ability to speak, according to Chanakya. It is only humans who can voice their thoughts and opinions.

Humans and the godly ones

People wish for heaven, irrespective of their religion. Many of us believe that true happiness is in heaven, where everything is available in plenty—food, entertainment, pleasure, etc. There is no need to struggle anymore. But those who are spiritual and godly wish for liberation from this cycle of birth and death. So everyone wishes for something they don't have. No one is above desires.

2.46

**If you want liberation
As if poison, forsake the objects of pleasure
Drink forgiveness, mercy, purity of mind,
And truthfulness as if they are nectar**

What is your objective and purpose in life? Some may seek wealth, some pleasure, others name and fame. But there are some people who seek liberation (*moksha*) as their ultimate goal. For such people, Chanakya gives tips on what to do and what to avoid to achieve what they desire.

Poison

Those who are the seekers of *moksha* should forsake worldly pleasures as if they are poison. Detachment is the way forward for those who want to be free from the endless cycle of rebirths. When we chase material possessions, our minds get diverted from God. The path to liberation is through God, so the seekers of *moksha* should aim for God and God alone.

Drink

Symbolically, Chanakya says that instead of drinking poison, drink (develop) the values of forgiveness, mercy, purity of the mind and truthfulness. Absorb these qualities like they are nectar. These qualities are the tools one must carry on the journey to attain *moksha*. Such seekers alone attain liberation—the ultimate destination.

2.47

In whose heart
The love for all kindles and abides
His troubles vanish and success ensues
In all his strides

What ensures success in everything you do? It is love for all. Yes, a heart that is compassionate and caring will never be unsuccessful in any endeavor; success will follow such a person. Many say that it is hard work, strategy and various other factors that bring in accomplishments in one's life. But in addition to these, empathy is an essential quality for achieving success.

Love for all

A loving person is kind. He is gentle. Such a person is empathetic and considerate of others. Develop such a loving attitude towards those around you. To be loving towards others and being loved in return is a great accomplishment.

Trouble vanishes and success follows

As if by magic, the troubles of those who are kind and loving vanish. It is quite heartwarming to note that when you work for others, others work for your benefit too. And those who consider the troubles of others as their own, where is the need to worry? He is sure to be successful for he is not alone; he is loved by many and they will lead him to success. Develop a kind and loving heart and you will attract more like-minded people who will lift you to greater heights of success.

2.48

The physical body is mortal
Wealth doesn't last forever
Death hangs over one's head always
Therefore, dutifully, one should indulge in piety

Nothing is permanent in life. The physical body is mortal, and one day it will perish. Wealth too doesn't last forever. Then what should you be doing? What should be your ultimate aim? What should you work towards that will accompany you beyond this life? Chanakya has the answer.

Death hangs over one's head

Like the sword of Damocles, death hangs over the heads of the living, always. You will never know when you will leave this world. Accept the fact that death is always near you; it is your constant companion as long as you breathe. However, do not be afraid of death. Instead, make your days count; start planning for all the things you want to accomplish before you die.

Indulge in piety

Be pious and polite. By being so, you will gather merits for the next life. We call it *punya*. Whatever you amass during your lifetime remains on earth when you die. Only your merits get carried forward into your next birth (according to Hindu beliefs). So do more good deeds and gather good karma for eternity.

2.49

Though the ocean filled with gems is its father
And Lakshmi is its sister
Yet the conch goes begging.
Well, without giving one gains nothing

Chanakya provides a wonderful example here about the merits of giving. The ocean is filled with gems; deep within the sea are treasures aplenty. But the conch which is born of the same ocean bed goes begging to others in the hands of *sadhus*. What is the reason behind this? Because nothing is gained without giving.

Ocean as father, Lakshmi as sister

Very symbolically Chanakya relates the conch with the ocean and goddess Lakshmi. A conch is found in the ocean, so it becomes the son of Varuna, the god of oceans. Likewise, goddess Lakshmi is considered the daughter of the ocean in the *Puranas*. Why then does a conch, which is born into such a rich and noble family, have to go begging?

Learn to give

The primary reason why the conch ends up begging is because of its selfishness, says Chanakya. Even though it lives in the seabed, it guards its wealth (precious pearls) without sharing it. So as a punishment, the conch ends up in the hands of sadhus seeking alms. Chanakya uses this analogy to show that without giving, one gains nothing. So start by sharing what you have with the less fortunate and you will receive more and more, be it wealth or goodwill, in return. Another message Chanakya conveys through this example is that even those people who belong to rich families should practice philanthropy.

2.50

**Truth is my mother, knowledge is my father,
Virtue is my brother, compassion is my friend,
Peace is my wife, forgiveness is my son,
These six I keep as my kinsmen**

Your family plays a great part in your growth and character. An exemplary family gives birth to great men and women and a wayward family contributes nothing but grief to society. So it is important to have the support of the family with good values to become a good human and a great person. Chanakya outlines the six values one must have by linking them to close family members.

Mother, father and brother

Truth should be your mother. Everything within you should be born from the womb of truth, and that should be your foundation. Knowledge should be your father; it should guide you. Only with the help of knowledge can one achieve greatness in life. And virtue should be your sibling; it should support you, like a brother.

Friend, wife and son

A person's wife is his long-term companion. Chanakya says here that your life-long companion should be peace, so keep peace close to you as you would keep your spouse. And who should be the ideal son born of you—forgiveness. Never carry hatred in your heart; it affects the person who carries it the most. And when you have these six relatives, you will become an unstoppable force. After all, a family is the best support system one can ask for!

2.51

Whatever is distant,
Difficult to accomplish or unworkable
That can be accomplished through penance
For penances are unimpeachable

The world is a mystery; most of us do not understand its working. We think that what we see is the only world that exists. But the world we live in is controlled by many invisible factors and natural laws.

Chanakya in this *neeti* tell us to invoke the mighty forces of nature though penance to accomplish those feats that are otherwise not humanly possible.

Things that are distant and unworkable

There are limits to human abilities. Some tasks you have to finish may appear difficult or impossible. You may not be able to find a favourable solution to your problems. That is because your understanding of the universe is limited. You may feel that you do not have enough talent and resources to accomplish your goals. However, according to Chanakya, if you invoke your inner powers, you can achieve anything you want to.

Penance is the way to achieve results

How does one achieve the unachievable? Chanakya says it is through penance. In Sanskrit, it is called *tapasya* or even *upasana*. All you have to do is determine a goal and set your intentions towards it. Through your commitment and focus, through the power of your mind and constant meditation, you can achieve what is not otherwise possible.

2.52

**Delicious food and the potency to eat
Beautiful women and the potency to romance
Wealth in abundance and the potency to give
These're not the rewards of ordinary penance**

There are both fortunate and unfortunate people in this world. Chanakya in this *neeti* is advising you to count your blessings. One can wish for many things but only a few people get what they wish for. Chanakya gives a few instances where a person is blessed with more than he deserves. If you ever become so fortunate, remember you are among the lucky few.

Delicious food and the ability to eat

Hunger is common for any living being. But only a few get to enjoy plenty of delicious food. Even if you get food, there is no guarantee that you will enjoy it. If one is ill and does not have an appetite, what is the use of getting delicious food? There are many rich people in the world who can afford top chefs to cook for them, but they also suffer from all kinds of ailments, like high cholesterol, high BP, diabetes, etc., and cannot eat what they want. What's the use of all the wealth if one cannot even have a meal of one's choice? So getting food and having the potency to eat it is a matter of God's grace.

Beauty and wealth

One may be surrounded by beauty, yet if one isn't a romantic, what's the point? Similarly, only the fortunate ones have all the wealth and the heart to share it with the less fortunate. The ability to enjoy life and share it with others is not something to be taken for granted. So if you are in the lucky few, enjoy the fact that you still have some choice in the matters that matter the most in this material world.

2.53

The previous life's practices
Of charity, learning and austerity
Continue to be cultivated in this life
Through the link of this present life with the
previous ones

According to the law of karma, all living beings have had many
previous births and there will be many more. It is a continuous
process of evolution from one birth to the other. You keep carrying
forward the consequences of your actions from one birth to the
other. So Chanakya is advising here to be careful about your every
activity, because you will have to take the good and the bad of your
actions with you to the next life too.

Practices in the previous life/lives

We are all products of our past. If we have done something good,
acquired merits, we take birth in noble, rich and spiritual families.
Lord Krishna in chapter eight, verse six of the Bhagavad Gita says,
"Whatever state of being one remembers when he quits his body,
that state he will attain without fail."

Charity, learning and austerity

Keeping the above point in mind, you should carry on doing
good work. Chanakya points out here three things to do that will
add value in every birth you take: 1) Charity—One should share
one's wealth with others. Hoarding wealth doesn't help in your
karmic journey. Give it away and reap the benefits, in this life and
in others. 2) Learning—One must study the scriptures and learn
spiritual values. This will help one evolve from a human being
into a spiritual being. 3) Austerity—Through self-control and living

without overindulgences, one will be able to go further, deeper in one's inner journey.

Linking this life with the others

According to Hindu belief, the quality of one's next birth is based on one's actions in the present life. So if some of your desires were unfulfilled in this birth, you will get a chance to fulfill them in your next birth. Similarly, if you have gathered significant spiritual merits in this birth, you will move further in your spiritual journey, in your next life also.

2.54

**One who abandons the sure thing
And runs after the transient
Losses the permanent
And, as well, by itself, vanishes the impermanent**

You need to develop the ability to think critically. In our ancient Indian scriptures the ability to discriminate was called *vivek*. In life, one should be able to differentiate between right and wrong, permanent and impermanent. Everything is subjected to change. So then what is permanent among the impermanent? What is changeless in change? One has to develop the quality of *vivek* to understand this difference.

Running behind the transient

Many people spent their entire lives running behind transient goals. They fail to understand that things come and go. The tragedy of human life is that we want to keep running behind things we think will bring us joy. But by the time we acquire them, they lose their value in our eyes. We then run after the next thing, person or situation that we "think" will make us happy. This is an endless journey of sorrow.

Lose the permanent

By running behind the transient, you stand to lose the permanent. You do not value what is already yours, and what you run behind does not value you. The world doesn't owe you anything, so be thankful for the good in your life.

The impermanent vanishes by itself

Even if you get what you want, with time that will also be taken away from you. Your most near and dear ones, your friends and relatives — all of them will pass away one day. So why not make the best of what you have when you have it! Later there is no point regretting the time lost which you could have spent with those you love.

2.55

**The wise man should not be anxious about food
He should be anxious to be engaged only in dharma
Food for each man is created at his birth itself**

We are used to worrying. But what we should be doing is thinking. To replace worry with right thinking. Develop this art of thinking. Chanakya in the *Arthashastra* calls this art *aanvikshiki*. Why worry over small things in life when you can focus on thinking about higher things? Over here Chanakya gives an example of one of the basic necessities of life — food. But he is telling you not to worry about it.

Don't worry about food

It is rather strange that people love worrying. Worrying can easily become a habit and can be quite difficult to give up even if you try. It takes practice and patience to remain calm in the face of adversities. For ages man has been worrying about his food and survival. And even today he spends a lot of time and effort to ensure he and his family will not die of starvation. But Chanakya says not to fret. You will have enough food to survive.

Righteousness

So what do you do when you finally manage to free your mind from worrying? Think about something better and greater. As human beings we are able to use our intellectual abilities for higher, spiritual purposes. So think about how you can lead a virtuous and righteous life. This is essentially thinking about *dharma*. Ancient Indians would contemplate and discuss *dharma* much more than any other aspect of life.

Nature will provide

As far as food and other necessities of life are concerned, Mother Nature will take care of them. When a child is born, nature provides milk through the mother. The child gets what he requires without him worrying about it. In the same manner, our food needs are taken care of by nature. Trust in God and the natural laws. Therefore, instead of worrying whether you will get your next meal or not, think about how you can have a noble and value-based life.

2.56

Transient is wealth, breath, life,
And the place of dwelling
Amongst the transient and intransient things of the world
Only piety is everlasting

Nothing in this world is permanent. Everything comes and goes. Chanakya is telling us about our transient world with examples here. He also advises us to develop a sense of detachment.

Transient things

There are three things that are transient—wealth, life and home. Wealth will come and go. Money is a strange thing; it is never sticks to one person. At times it grows and suddenly it can disappear too. Also, breath of all living being comes and goes without any notice. One moment you could be alive and the next, dead. Nothing is permanent.

If you take a stock of your life, you may have moved homes many times. At some point, you may have also moved cities or towns. A man's dwelling is not permanent.

The only permanent thing

While change is the only constant, there is only one thing that is permanent—piety. One who is pious will develop other good qualities like compassion, empathy, sensibility and sincerity. Only qualities stay with a person for long, not people or material things.

2.57

Charity puts an end to poverty
Righteous conduct to misery
Discretion to ignorance
And scrutiny to fear

Chanakya talks about how certain qualities affect our lives. We can tackle one negative with a positive. He is giving us four examples here. So if you want to be optimistic in life, you need to develop the quality of positive thinking. An upbeat person will look at life very differently as compared to a skeptical person and will be an inspiration to others as well.

Charity puts an end to poverty

This statement is contradictory to what most of us believe. We have been told that one becomes rich by gathering wealth, saving every penny. But according to Chanakya, one has to give, to become rich. When one develops the quality of charity, poverty vanishes from one's life. Give to those who deserve your kindness and nature will return your generosity multifold.

Righteousness triumphs misery

Chanakya advises us to remain humble during bad times. When you practice gratitude, you develop humility and goodness. And such a virtuous person automatically thinks of God and comes out of any state of distress easily.

Knowledge effaces ignorance

The only remedy for ignorance is knowledge. So when you do not know what to do in a certain situation, it is best to seek the opinion of the experts. In the same way, to know the facts about a certain situation, the best way to tackle it is to do thorough research. These facts could be eye-opening.

Faith over fear

Fear is a natural emotion which can be overcome with faith. For example, when a child is scared, he starts crying. Hearing this, his mother comes running to him. As soon as she lifts him up, the child calms down; his fear disappears. This is because of the faith the child has in the mother. Faith can conquer any type of fear.

CHAPTER 3

WORLDLY WISDOM

3.1

He who has failed to attain
Either virtue, wealth, satisfaction of desires or salvation
Lives a useless life
Like a nipple hanging on the neck of a goat

According to Indian Vedic literature, we have four goals—
purushartha or "the object of human pursuit"—to achieve in
life. They are *dharma* (right conduct), *artha* (wealth), *kama*
(gratification) and *moksha* (liberation). Only if we attain all these
four in our lifetime can we say we have lived a complete life.

Right conduct and wealth

The very foundation of society is based on righteous conduct and
moral values. A morally corrupt society is as good as hell. Also,
without right values and proper conduct it is difficult for a person
to achieve lasting success. So living a virtuous life should be your
first goal. Then you need to create wealth. *Artha* refers to having a
career, making a living, economic prosperity, financial security, etc.
To be worldly successful, one needs to be wealthy as well.

Gratification and liberation

Who says one should not enjoy life? We all have many desires and
it's better to fulfill those desires so that you do not have regrets.
Only be sure that these desires are fulfilled through *dharma*. Also,
be careful that these desires don't lead to greed. Finally comes
liberation—the ultimate goal of any soul, freedom from the karmic
cycle of life and death.

A person who has failed to acquire even one of these four goals is
not living a fruitful life at all. Such a person's life is like a nipple

hanging from the neck of a goat—without any milk and useless. So pursue these four goals and make them your priority.

3.2

**On this earth there are three gems indeed:
Water, foodgrains and fine words
But mere pebbles are branded
As gems by the half-witted**

There are three gems in this world—water, foodgrains and fine words, says Chanakya. All others are just pebbles—whether it's the new car, a vacation home or simply a billion dollars. However, ignorant people give more importance to these small pebbles and treat them as gems, giving them priority over kindness and commonsense.

Water, foodgrains and fine words

What do human beings really want in life in order to survive? First and foremost in that list is water. Water is the source of life. Next comes food. Without food and water, life cannot sustain itself. So it's important that we protect the water and land resources instead of polluting our rivers and filling up available land with concrete buildings. Finally, one should not forget the importance of pleasing, healing words. Words can transform people—break them or make them—so choose your words carefully. Be the person who speaks to inspire and not belittle.

Half-witted people

People who consider material gains as their ultimate goal are dim-witted. They fail to see what's of utmost importance to survive. If tomorrow the bank seizes your home, your credit card is blocked and your partner walks out on you, you will be able to continue with your life. But if there is no water to drink or food to eat, you will die in a few days. It's the same with words. Kind words inspire, and give people hope to live. However, a harsh word uttered carelessly can crush a person's spirit; it can extinguish his will. Use gentle words with people and they will in return speak gently to you. So be wise, choose what is important to survive in the long run.

3.3

The world, a bitter tree,
Has two nectar-filled fruits hanging from it:
Sweet, wise words and
The company of good people

The world can be harsh. Not all events in life make us happy. We often feel sad and dull. Chanakya compares the world to a bitter tree. However, he says this bitter tree has two sweet fruits—pleasant, wise words and the company of good people.

Sweet, wise words

Words have the power to hurt and to soothe depending on how you use them. In a world filled with challenges, the impact of a pleasant conversation is invaluable. You may not realise it, but one kind word could change someone's entire day. Pleasant and comforting words are like balm to a tired and calloused soul. On the other hand, even though the tongue doesn't have any bones, it's strong enough to break hearts. So be careful with words; use them gently and to uplift others, not to hurt and humiliate them.

The company of good people

The Sanskrit word for a get-together with good people is *satsang*. *Sat* means good and *sangh* means company. According to motivational speaker Jim Rohn, "You are the average of the five people you spend the most time with." Those who keep the company of the good and wise will always be protected from the sorrows of this world. They will be inspired to live a virtuous life and do good deeds, which will in turn lead to success and earn them good karmic credit. In short, you should choose your friends very carefully.

3.4

Goodness is the ornament of beauty
The glory of a family is gentleness
Perfection is the crown of learning
Utility is the beauty of affluence

What is real beauty? What is the true glory of a family? What is the sign of education? What is the real value of affluence? Chanakya gives us the answers to these questions in this verse.

Beauty and family glory

Goodness is the ornament that enhances beauty. You may be beautiful physically, but if you don't have a good heart, no one will value you. So be good-natured and your charms will increase manifold; you will be seen as beautiful in others' eyes. The glory of a family is in the gentleness of its members. If a family is arrogant, it will lose all respect even if the family members are rich and powerful. Keep this in mind and raise your own family to be kind.

Learning and affluence

The mark of a learned person is in the perfection of his work. Only a master will be able to deliver perfection. Superficial learning will reflect in the imperfection of one's work. So be thorough in whatever you aim to study. Likewise, affluence is only good when it is useful. What's the point of having loads of money if it can't be used for good deeds? If one is fortunate enough to have some extra dough, use it to help others who aren't as lucky. Money kept in the locker is just a wad of paper; only when it is used does it have value.

3.5

Merit makes a person great
Not sitting on a high seat
Does a crow become Garuda
By perching on top of the palace?

What makes a person great? Certainly not his designation or credentials. It is only merit (*punya*) one has garnered that makes one truly great. Chanakya uses the metaphor of a crow trying to be Garuda to explain this point.

The power of merit

A person's greatness is not measured in terms of his position. A person becomes great because of his character, because of his moral values and virtuous behaviour. If a person becomes the CEO of a company, does that automatically make him a great person? Real greatness is acquired through good work alone.

A crow cannot become Garuda

Garuda is the vehicle of Lord Vishnu and is therefore considered the king of birds. He is portrayed in the *Puranas* as a valiant and graceful bird who can fly through different worlds in a matter of seconds. But can an ordinary crow perching on top of a palace achieve the glory of the mighty Garuda?

3.6

**As gold is examined four ways by
Rubbing, cutting, heating and beating
Likewise, a man should be tested in four ways:
His self-sacrifice, his conduct, his virtues and actions**

Gold, the most-valued precious metal, is tested repeatedly to ascertain its authenticity. Similarly, Chanakya says that a man should be tested using four parameters to find his worth.

Testing gold

All that glitters is not gold, of course, and the goldsmith knows it very well. So whenever someone approaches him to sell gold, he uses four methods to test the metal first—he rubs it against the touchstone, cuts it to make sure the metal inside is also gold, heats and hits it to determine its strength.

Testing a man's worth

Like gold, a man can be tested to know his true worth as well. The parameters should be his willingness for self-sacrifice, his conduct, his qualities and his actions. The level of self-sacrifice a person exhibits will show how much he is willing to give up his comforts to achieve a higher goal. Conduct determines whether a person is calm amidst difficult circumstances. The third important factor is

the values that he hold dear in life. Lastly, a person's actions reflect
his thinking.

3.7

Like the drops of water falling slowly and steadily
Fill the pitcher
Knowledge, virtue and wealth
Are gathered in a similar way

Every effort counts, no matter how small. You should not desert a
goal midway because it looks daunting to achieve. For example, if
you keep walking, concentrating only on putting one foot in front of
the other, soon you will reach your destination. Without realising,
you can even climb a mountain this way.

Drops of water fill a pitcher

An ocean is just a collection of millions of water drops. A pot too can
be filled with drop after drop of water. The vessel decides how much
it can contain. So when you notice a successful person, remember
that he did not become successful overnight. He made it by putting
in hard work over a long period of time.

Knowledge, virtue and wealth

The process of gathering knowledge, virtue and wealth is similar.
Anyone can gain knowledge by reading books, researching
important information, meeting wise people and by furthering
one's own intellectual horizon. Only a person who has walked the
path of righteousness constantly, conducting himself with dignity
and integrity, can be called virtuous. And so is the case with wealth

creation. Every penny counts. Only a scrupulous person who spends carefully and saves regularly can one day become rich. Trivial everyday actions carry magical powers if done correctly and over a period of time. That's why persistence matters. Someone who quits at the first obstacle will never achieve success. If you commit to something, stick to it till the end.

3.8

**Nothing equals rainwater
No strength like one's own
Nothing matches the light of the eyes
And no wealth is dearer than food grains**

Some things in this world have no parallels. They are unmatched in their quality. Chanakya gives us four benchmarks in this verse.

Rainwater and one's own strength

Rainwater is the purest form of water there is; it falls straight from the depths of the sky and is untouched by man. During a draught, rain is the only hope for survival. It is as valuable as *amrit* itself. The greatest quality in a person is willpower or *atma bal*; the power of the spirit inside us. Nothing is unachievable for a person with tremendous willpower.

Light of the eyes and food grains

Nothing matches the gift of sight. It is because of our eyesight we're able to enjoy the world around us as we do. Sight is one of the most important senses a living being possesses. You could be standing in a room awash in the light of a hundred bulbs, but if you're blind, what's the use? And no gem is more valuable than food grains for when you're hungry, you cannot eat precious stones. Only the truly hungry know the value of food and it is not to be taken for granted. Food provides us energy and vitality. Food sustains us. You could have all the wealth in the world, but if you were to go without food for a couple of days, you could die. What use is such wealth? According to the Upanishads, *Annam Brahma* — food is God.

3.9

Poverty is removed through work
Sins expunged through prayers
Silence quells quarrels
Wakefulness dispels fears

You can overcome any situation in life if you set your mind to it. Whatever be the circumstances, there is a solution. Chanakya, being a strategist and a teacher, shares tips on how to overcome troubles in everyday life.

Poverty and sins

Not all of us are rich. But there is no need to worry. Poverty can be erased with hard work. Don't blame the government or other authorities for keeping people poor. If there is a will, there is a way. So if you are ready to do backbreaking work, money will find its way into your wallet. There is nothing wrong in being born poor, but if a person dies poor it is because he hasn't worked hard enough. There are many inspiring rags-to-riches stories all around us. For example, take the case of Dhirubhai Ambani — he started off as a labourer in Yemen at 16 and died a billionaire. He built Reliance Industries, one of the largest conglomerates in the world today, in a single lifetime.

A sinner can atone for his sins through prayers. According to Chanakya, a heartfelt prayer is as good as asking for forgiveness; it will expunge one's sins.

Quarrels and Fear

How can one avoid quarrels? Try observing silence. Many think it is a good idea to jump in and try to mediate a dispute when it breaks out. But the best strategy is to remain silent. Listen carefully instead of speaking. One will be able to gather all the facts of the issue from all concerned and be more equipped to solve a problem. A silent person is more respected than a chatterbox, and his opinion will be valued in time.

Vigilance dispels fear. Those who are alert and conscious will be prepared to face any emergency that comes their way. They are free to live a fear-free life. On the contrary, those who are careless will be plagued by difficulties arising from their own negligent behavior. As a result, such people will always be living in fear of bad things happening to them.

3.10

**Grieve not for the past
Worry not for the future
Wise men only deal
With the present moment**

Most of us live in regret of the past or expectations of the future. In thinking about the past and the future, the beautiful reality of the present is lost. It's best to come to terms with the fact that you cannot do anything about the past, it is over. In the same way, you cannot do anything about the future, it is yet to arrive. You can only work in the present to make your future beautiful and better.

One's past and future

Grieve not for the past because you have no control over it. Even if you have made some mistakes there is no point in sitting and brooding over them. They are behind you. Better to learn from your mistakes and move on. In the same way, stop worrying about the future. It is not in your control. Rather, make plans and work hard towards the future you want. Whatever happens, know that the results of your toils are not in your hands.

The present is for the wise

The wise know only the present matters because it is the moment for action. You cannot correct your past nor can you go into the future and realize your dreams. You only have 'now' to act. And when you put your best foot forward and make the best of the present moment, know that success will follow sooner or later.

3.11

**The one who prepares for the future
And he who is alert and clever
Will both be lucky and happy but
The one who wholly depends on luck will be ruined**

In this *neeti*, Chanakya talks about the benefits of being alert in life. The lucky ones, according to Chanakya, are the ones who prepare for the future. And luck blesses them for their planning with success.

Prepare for the future, be alert

The ones who are constantly working toward the future have a positive attitude. Likewise, those who are always alert and clever do not pass up any opportunity. They know when to strike and they always strike gold. Luck favours those who are prepared to be successful. So make plans and be ready for your imminent success; have no doubt about it.

Those who only depend on luck

Vigilant people make their own destiny. Those who pass through life with a 'what will be, will be' attitude are left behind. You do have a say in how your life turns out; it's just a matter of being prepared for all situations. If Plan A doesn't work, there are 25 more alphabets in the English language. Keep trying till you reach your destination; till you fulfill your goal.

3.12

**One whose knowledge is confined to books
And those whose wealth is in the hands of others
Can use neither the knowledge nor such wealth
When the need arises**

What is the use of bookish knowledge? What is the use of your wealth that is in someone else's hands? In times of need, both are useless.

Knowledge confined to books

Many boast about the number of books or famous authors they have read. Does that make them intelligent? Not necessarily. Books document knowledge. One can definitely acquire insights from books. But nothing can compare to the practical knowledge a person acquires by going out into the world and experiencing life firsthand. This knowledge will always be with you, ready to be used when the opportunity arise, unlike bookish knowledge. Along with reading books, go out and explore the world to expand your mind and gain practical wisdom.

Wealth in others' hands

One should help others in need and lending money is one easy way to do so. But how many borrowers do return the money on time? Don't we all have a friend or two who have borrowed from us a while ago and still haven't returned the money? Asking to return borrowed cash is embarrassing to most people, so one doesn't says anything until crisis occurs. Even so, there is no guarantee of getting the money back. So what's the use of having earned wealth and not being able to use it in times of need? Therefore, Chanakya advises us to be street-smart. Park your wealth somewhere safe so that when the time comes you can use it—with a trusted bank or in a safe investment scheme, where your money will also earn you interest for as long as you keep it locked in.

3.13

**Lives he who strives
For merit and good deeds;
Without merits and good deeds
Life is useless, indeed**

Many people are seemingly alive but are actually dead inside. They live their lives without purpose. The one who truly lives is the one who strives.

Merit and good deeds

So what should you strive for and work hard towards? To achieve *punya* through good deeds. For this, you need to live a life of sacrifice and service. Through this lifestyle, you will accrue merits which will be with you in this life and the next life.

Life is useless without purpose

There are some who work and strive very hard. But they do so not for *punya*, but for personal gains, name and fame. According to Chanakya, such a life is useless and there is nothing worth admiring in such people who are selfish and mean-spirited.

3.14

**Troublesome for Sita was her great beauty
For Ravana it was too much pride
Bali was bound because of excessive generosity
So one should avoid the excess of anything**

You need to practice living a life of moderation, a life of balance. Chanakya's life itself was about the right balance of power—its use for the benefit of others. In this verse, he gives a few examples of the problems one faces when anything is in excess.

Sita's beauty and Ravana's pride

Sita was a beautiful princess. Her loveliness attracted Ravana, the demon king of Lanka. He kidnapped her and took her away from her husband Rama. Ravana was very powerful, but his excessive pride finally became the cause of his fall. Rama and his army defeated and killed Ravana and freed Sita from captivity. Instead of concentrating on beauty alone, one should try to develop other qualities as well, which will help one have a more wholesome life experience. And being egoistic never helps anyone. There is an old saying: pride comes before a fall. So beware of being too proud of yourself.

Bali's problem was his excess generosity

Bali (Mahabali) was a very noble *asura* king. He was admired by all. His greatest quality was his generosity. But even excess generosity is not good. When Vishnu appeared in front of him in the form of a Brahmin and asked for alms, Bali gave away all the three worlds under his control. Vishnu banished him to *Patal* for eternity. So be careful of becoming over-generous. People tend to take advantage of the kind-hearted.

3.15

Results depend on the action
Following the trail of acts forms the intellect
Even so, sensible and noble people
Get in on the act only after considering it well

How does one become intelligent? And what do intelligent people do? The answer to these questions is given in this verse. It is very clear that actions lead to results. The kind of actions you perform determine the quality of results you get.

The trail of acts forms the intellect

We are what we do. For example, when you do something repeatedly, you gather experience. These trails lead to the development of intelligence. You can also learn from the experience of others, you only need to observe closely. So try to improve your mind through yours as well as others' experiences.

Sensible people think first

Even though action is required to get results, it is best to think before acting. Always think of the pros and cons of a particular activity and only when convinced about the results, go ahead with it. Therefore, sensible and noble people give careful thought before acting on any situation so that they get favourable results.

3.16

If you wish to gain control of the world
Then keep the following fifteen, which are prone to wander,
From getting the upper hand over you: the five sense objects,
The five sense organs and organs of activity

Do you want to be a world conqueror. Then you need to first win over yourself. Acquiring self-control is possible only if you gain control over your senses.

Gain control over the world

It is possible to become a world conquer. For this, great concentration is required in a chosen field. If you carefully study the lives of people who are champions on the world platform, you will notice that they have achieved their greatness by gaining mastery over one particular field.

Keep those 15 distractors in check

The human mind is like a field and it is continuously grazed on by various thoughts. Thoughts can become chaotic at times. No task can be achieved without concentration. When it comes to shining at the international level, one needs top-notch focus. For this, all the sensory organs need to be in control. Having mastery over 15 of them, namely the five sense objects (objects of sight, sound, smell, taste, and touch), the five sense organs (ears, eyes, nose, tongue and skin) and the organs of activity (hands, feet, mouth, generative and excretory organs), is of utmost important for anyone who is serious about achieving world-class recognition.

3.17

**Consider repeatedly the following:
The right time, right friends, the right place,
Right means of income, right ways of spending,
And what your real strength is**

To be successful, you need to take note of certain things in life. These particulars, when chosen well, will render you the power to attain what you wish to. In this *neeti*, Chanakya tells us what they are.

The right time, friends and place

You must be familiar with the phrase 'In the right place at the right time.' Luck favours those who are in the scene of action at the right time. Add the right kind of friends to this mixture and you have the winning formula. To court success, one needs to go in the right direction and who better to guide a person in that direction than his best friends? Those who enjoy good, influential company get inspired and do well in life as opposed to those who hang out with people with no drive. If you are serious about your growth, you need to network with the right kind of people who can help you with your journey. So choose wisely when you select your friends.

Right means of income, the right way of spending and what your strength is

Earn only through the right means. Crooked ways will catch up with you. You will then have a hefty price to pay. Live honestly and you need not worry about anything. This fear-free way of life gives one power. Those who lead honourable lives will alwaysbe influential in society. Also, be careful how you spend your money. Money is a double-edged sword; it can be a blessing and a burden, depending on how it is used. Save for tomorrow. The one who is financially well off is free to chase other goals. Otherwise, one will always be in race to just survive.

In the same way, know what your real strength is. Understanding your strength and weaknesses will give you a better idea of who you are and what you are capable of. Know where you draw your power from. A man who doesn't know his own strength is not living life to his fullest potential.

3.18

Purity of speech, of the mind, of the senses,
And a compassionate heart
Are the qualities one need
To rise to a divine platform

Who doesn't like to be closer to God? But to achieve this, you need to first take care of a few things. Let's take a look at those things that will help you get nearer to the divine.

Purity of speech, mind and senses

See no evil, hear no evil, speak no evil and you will be closer to God than ever before. Only a pure soul will be able to realise God.

A person who speaks nothing but the truth, a mind that is filled only with virtuous thoughts and senses that only pick up agreeable sensory input is on a higher, divine platform than other humans. Everything we see, hear and think becomes a part of us. So be mindful of what your senses perceive and your mind processes.

A compassionate heart

Above all, you need to be compassionate if you want to experience divine grace. We can soften other people's hardened hearts by treating them with love and care. Wise people strive to develop compassion and in the process develop saintly qualities and achieve self-realisation.

3.19

**The reckless spender, the homeless child,
the quarrel-monger,
The man who neglects his wife and is heedless in his actions
All these will soon come to ruination**

Living a good life is all about having principles. All actions have consequences. You should be careful about each step that you take; act only according to your moral principles. Chanakya here describes some characters who are destined to fail in life. Let's take a look at them.

Reckless spender, homeless child and the quarrel-monger

You should think twice before spending even a penny. Money doesn't grow on trees. Spend within your limits. There are people who spend their money first and then think about how to earn it back—all those who use their credit cards without a thought fall into this category. A life without money is tough, so protect your savings and think of ways to boost your income rather than spending it away.

Why Chanakya says a homeless urchin will end up in ruin is because he hasn't got anyone to protect him or teach him how to lead a decent life. Homeless children have only their wits to guard them against criminals and other delinquents. Such a harsh life at a young age pushes them onto the wrong side of the law.

A quarrel-monger is always looking for someone to lock horns with and all his energy is spent in fights. He doesn't have the time to focus on productive work and so his life is wasted.

The one who neglects his wife and is heedless in his actions

One's spouse should be one's best friend, one should treat him or her with care and respect. Some married people forget their marital status, and once out of the house pretend they don't have a partner. According to Chanakya, a person who doesn't treat his spouse right and is careless in his actions is destined for doom. Pay attention to the little things you do and say to your partner because they matter. It is important to adhere to certain moral values in married life to make the relationship simple and enjoyable.

3.20

**For a man who makes no use of his intellect
What use are books?
As for a blind man
What use is a mirror?**

Unless we apply our mind, nobody can really help us. Chanakya explains this truth beautifully in the above *neeti*.

Intellect and books

A person could own a huge library, but if he doesn't read the books in his collection, apply his intelligence on reading them, what's the point? Books are the stepping stones to knowledge. But books themselves are not enough. You need to understand, think and analyze what you read and only then will you gain the benefits of knowledge.

Blind man and mirror

It is useless for a blind person to look in the mirror. Chanakya uses this example to show that merely possessing something has no value if you don't know how to use it or can't use it. Be aware of your abilities and your blessings, and use them to your advantage.

3.21

One and the same object
Can be perceived in three different ways:
A woman is a mere body to a yogi,
An object of lust to the lustful
And is a piece of flesh to dogs

An object or a human being can be perceived differently by different people. The eye of the beholder is what matters. Chanakya chooses the example of a woman to explain this concept.

An ascetic and a lustful man

An ascetic has his heart set on God. He is devoted to the divine and is not interested in worldly things. To him, a woman is as good as a dead body. He feels no desire when looking at a woman. On the other hand, to a lustful man, a woman is just an object of desire.

A woman is just a piece of flesh to the dogs

When it comes to wild animals, gender doesn't matter; a woman is just a piece of flesh to be devoured. What difference does it make to a wild dog that in front of him stands a beautiful woman? His basic instinct is to hunt and satisfy his hunger. Through this example, Chanakya shows how different people perceive the same subject or object differently. To each his own, and remembering this is crucial to coexisting peacefully in the world.

3.22

**If the bees which seek the liquid oozing
from the head of a mad elephant
Are driven away by the flapping of his ears
Then the elephant has only lost the ornament on his head
The bees are quite happy in the lotus-filled lake**

Miscreants are happy wherever they are, only their victims suffer. A beautiful verse explains Chanakya's philosophy on this matter.

Ear-flapping of a mad elephant

The elephant, though large, is also a sensitive animal. A mere bee can irritate the mighty beast and turn him wild. Every bull elephant goes through a period of madness called *musth*, and during this time, a liquid is secreted from his ears and eyes. Bees are attracted to this discharge. Their buzzing irritates the animal and he starts frantically flapping his large ears to get rid of the bees. In the process, the elephant lets fall the ornaments that adorn its head (elephants are decorated during festival seasons in India). The bees move out of harm's way in mere seconds.

They flock to the lotuses

What happens to the swarm after the elephant drives them away? Nothing drastic, really. The elephant has lost his precious ornaments, but the bees fly to the lake and enjoy the nectar from lotuses. So be alert when interacting with a miscreant. If you are not careful, you stand to lose.

3.23

Those born blind cannot see
Similarly blind are those in the grip of lust
Proud men have no perception of evil
And those bent on getting rich see no sin in their actions

Sometimes we are so engrossed in trying to get what we want, we fail to see the right and wrong in our ways.

Lust is blinding

Those who are born blind have no idea of the brilliance of colours. In the throes of passion we stop thinking clearly. If you are not careful, misplaced feelings of lust could land you in trouble. It is important to be clear-headed in order to sail through life smoothly. Don't follow your passions blindly. Chanakya adds that a person who is arrogant cannot discriminate between right and wrong. So keep away from arrogance and lust; use your intelligence to choose what is best for you.

Proud men and those wanting to get rich

Arrogant people don't see any fault in their own behaviour. Such people are oblivious to their crossing the limits of decency. When you are in a group, you should know when to speak up and when to listen to others.

A man who wants to get rich quickly wouldn't mind taking an unethical path to achieve his goal. Money can blind a person's sense of right and wrong. Those who have no moral values don't get pricked by their conscience. Always do what is right without thinking about the benefits to you.

3.24

He who runs away from a dreadful calamity,
A foreign invasion, a terrible famine,
And the friendship of evil men is safe

Chanakya lists three situations in the above *neeti* where a person should only think about his own safety. He says the best plan of action in these situations is to escape for one's own good survival.

Calamities and foreign invasions

When calamities strike—be it natural or man-made—there is nothing you can do. No man can stand in the way of floods or earthquakes. Same is the case with foreign invasions. When enemies storm your native land, do not expect mercy; they are going to inflict atrocities on your fellow men and women. So in such situations, it's best to escape to safety as soon as possible.

Famine and the company of impious people

Hunger is a slow and horrible killer. No one will blame a refuge who runs away from famine. Chanakya compares this situation to one in which a person is in the company of immoral people. Here too the individual's best option is to flee, and find better opportunities to improve his life.

3.25

**A misdeed done by a swami becomes right
Even as the righteousness of a miscreant
sometimes is improper
As nectar proved fatal for Rahu
And poison adorned Shankar**

Who you are matters more than what you do. A good person's misstep can also turnout to be good in the end. Ultimately it is the person's intentions that matter rather than the act itself. Here Chanakya takes the example of Rahu and Lord Shiva to elaborate this point.

Swami and the miscreant

A *swami* here denotes a noble leader. Let's take the example of scientists today. Scientists the world over are conducting experiments in their fields to improve the future of mankind. During their experiments, many procedures fail. Only after multiple errors do they find the right solutions. What matters is their intention behind their actions. Despite the errors, ultimately good intentions lead to success.

On the other hand, a miscreant can even make a good thing into something bad. It's like a fly landing on a sweet dish of *prasadam*. A fly carries with it many germs and once it lands on the sweet, delicious offering, it's not fit for consumption anymore.

Rahu and Shankar

In the *Srimad Bhagavatam* Rahu consumes the nectar of immortality, *amrit*, which came out of churning the Ocean of Milk by *devas* and *asuras*. But instead of giving eternal life, it proved fatal for Rahu, an *asura*. He drank it out of turn. An angry Lord Vishnu cut his head off before the nectar could reach his stomach. Rahu's head survived, but without a body. During this churning, a pot of poison, *halahala*, came out of the ocean before the *amrit*. It had the potency to destroy the whole world. Both *devas* and *asuras* were terrified. They prayed to Lord Shiva to help them get rid of it. Shiva drank the poison to save the world. Instead of harming him, the poison merely turned his neck an amazing shade of blue, thus giving him the name *Neelkanth* or the Blue-throated One.

3.26

The power of the *Vipra* lies is his knowledge
The power of the king lies is his army
The power of the *Vaishya* is his money
The power of the *Shudra* is his humility

Our Vedic texts have classified society into four sections. The *Vipras* (Brahmins or teachers), kings (*Kshatriyas*, the ruling or warrior community), the *Vaishyas* (the business community or the wealth creators) and the *Shudras* (the working class). Each community has its unique skillset.

The power of Brahmins and kings

Brahmins are at the top of the Hindu caste system. For the wise man, his supremacy is in his knowledge. In Hinduism, Brahmins are considered the custodians of knowledge. It is their duty to guide their community on the right path.

Next in the hierarchy are the rulers. The might of the king is in his army; it is a symbol of his ability to protect his kingdom and people. The most powerful king is the one with the largest and the strongest army.

The power of *Vaishyas* and *Shudras*

The strength of the Vaishyas is finance. Their strength is money. They are responsible for building the economy and creating jobs.

At the lowest rung come the *Shudras*. Chanakya says that humility is their greatest virtue. When they work with sincerity and without ego, they help create an ethical and productive society.

For a society to prosper, these four classes must work in unison.

3.27

Knowledge is lost if it's not put into action
Man is lost in ignorance
An army is lost without a commander
A woman is lost without a husband

Knowledge is useful only if one can put it into practice. A man is similarly useless if he is steeped in ignorance. According to Chanakya, knowing what is best for oneself is the best way to live. He gives some examples in this verse.

Knowledge and man

Being theoretically equipped is an advantage only when one can use that theory in practice. Also, knowledge gets corroded if it's not put to use. And what is man without knowledge? It is only because of his intelligence and his ability to think that man is superior to other species.

Army and woman

What is an army without a commander? The commander is the leader; he decides when his soldiers should attack. He also keeps his army disciplined and under control.

Similarly, Chanakya says a woman is incomplete without a husband. Since this text was written more than two thousand years ago, it can now safely be modified to say that a person's life is incomplete without a partner. Life has to be shared to be enjoyed fully. It's comforting to have someone to share one's joys and sorrows and to support one's partner along the way.

3.28

The huge elephant is kept in restraint using a goad;
Is the goad as bulky as the elephant?
The lamp dispels darkness when lit;
Is the lamp as vast as darkness?
A mountain can crumble if struck by a thunderbolt;
Is the thunderbolt as big as the mountain?
Truly, the one whose power prevails is mighty
What's there in size?

Never take someone small in stature for granted. We don't know how powerful that person might be. Size is not a sign of might, as Chanakya proves in this *neeti* with many apt examples.

Elephant and goad; lamp and darkness

A domesticated elephant, as enormous as it is, is controlled by a simple goad. The goad is tiny compared to the size of the elephant, yet it helps control the elephant. So who is more powerful here, the elephant or the goad? A small lamp is all it takes to dispel darkness. But darkness is vast and a lamp is miniscule compared to it. However, a lamp helps to keep darkness at bay.

A thunderbolt can destroy a mountain

A mountain can stand erect for thousands of years, but if it's struck by a single thunderbolt, it could crumble like a molehill. Take the biblical story of David and Goliath. The giant Goliath is felled by a shepherd boy, David, with just a sling and a stone. Power is with the one who knows how to wield it. Chanakya was one such brilliant human being who could vanquish empires with his intelligence. So don't be awed by muscle power alone.

3.29

**A cuckoo's beauty is its voice
The beauty of a woman is her loyalty to her husband
Knowledge is the beauty of an ugly face
The ability to forgive is the ascetic's beauty**

What is beauty? Is beauty just about physical appearance? Chanakya has a much broader view of beauty and he shares it in this *neeti*.

The beauty of a cuckoo and a woman

The cuckoo is not a beautiful bird to look at. At times it is difficult to tell it apart from a crow. However, the cuckoo's voice is melodic and adds beauty to the bird. Likewise, Chanakya says that the beauty of a woman is in her chastity and loyalty to her husband. In the *Ramayana*, Sita's beauty was not flesh-bound but in her strong character. Her loyalty to Ram ultimately led to the destruction of Ravana.

The beauty of an ugly person and an ascetic

Learning is that virtue which makes even a plain-looking human being beautiful and interesting. When a person is well-educated, his physical attractiveness becomes irrelevant; he can effectively use his intelligence to impress people. For an ascetic who has renounced the material world, beauty lies in his ability to forgive others.

3.30

**The wisdom that emerges
Out of repentance
If that comes about before time
Who will not be prosperous?**

Life is strange. You learn from your experiences. You do not have to go through these experiences repeatedly to learn from them.

Wisdom from repentance

Intelligent people learn from their mistakes and use them as stepping stones to success. If you have committed an error, find out what went wrong, try your best to salvage the situation and move on. Repent your foolish actions but don't cry over your past. At times mistakes are beneficial because they teach you many new lessons.

Learning the lessons before time

Who wouldn't be prosperous if no one committed mistakes and knew the answers to solve difficult situations? Chanakya imagines a world where everybody already knows the lessons of life and lives accordingly. A happy world, indeed.

3.31

The moon, who is sweet like nectar and the god of medicine
Who is immortal like the *amrit* and resplendent
Still wanes when in the presence of the sun
Who doesn't feel inferior when staying in someone
else's house?

Being in another man's shadows is difficult, even for the moon,
explains Chanakya in this profound *neeti*.

The moon's energy

In mythology, the moon is considered the god of medicine. His
energy is cool and soothing; it is sweet like nectar. He is also
immortal, like the *amrit*. His aura is resplendent. Poets and lovers
adore the moon and sing his praises. He is loved by all because of
his gentleness.

Living in someone else's abode

Even the shining moon will lose his luster when the sun appears.
In broad daylight, the moon is invisible. Similarly, when you stay in
someone's house for a long time, you lose your independence and
feel obliged to the host. When you start comparing yourself with
others, you will lose your charisma and feel inferior. You feel as if
you are not doing well in life if you can't even put a roof over your
head. Also, certain situations could lead to resentment. It is best to
lead an independent life for your own peace of mind.

3.32

Poverty is overcome with fortitude
Dirty clothes by keeping them clean
Raw food by heating it
And ugliness by good character

Most of our dilemmas have solutions if we look for them.

Poverty and dirty clothes

Poverty is not a permanent state; it can be overcome with courage. Take responsibility for your life. Learn to face adversities head-on without blaming others. With hard work and persistence, anybody can accumulate wealth. It is the same case with dirty clothes. A thorough wash will make the grime disappear and the clothes will look and smell as good as new.

Raw food and ugliness

Raw food is difficult to digest. One could die from food poisoning if the food is not cooked properly. But the same food turns tasty once it is cooked.

A plain-looking fellow can become charismatic if he develops his personality. Always keep in mind that a good character is more valuable than good looks. Looks may or may not guarantee respect but an excellent disposition is always revered.

3.33

Virtues are admired everywhere
Not the wealth, however great
Isn't the full moon more adored
Than the moon that is lean but immaculate?

What is more important—to gain money or respect? Many think
that money is the most difficult to gain. However, if you know the
technique to make money, it's possible to make a lot more of it. On
the other hand, respect is difficult to gain and maintain.

Virtues

A virtuous person is respected everywhere. Money will come and
go, but virtues stay on with a person forever. Though, you may be
wealthy, to gain respect, you need to be virtuous. Concentrate your
efforts on maintaining high moral standards. The more people start
respecting you and appreciating you, the more opportunities will
come your way. If you are talented, you can turn these opportunities
into profitable ones.

Full moon

A full moon is adored more as compared to the half-moon or the
crescent moon, even though a crescent moon is blemish-free. Poets
sing praises of the full moon and many cultures celebrate festivals
to honour it. Chanakya uses the full moon as a metaphor for the
merits of a person.

RADHAKRISHNAN PILLAI

3.34

[A person's] Conduct talks of the family
Language identifies the region
Friendship by warmth and affection
And physique points to nutrition

One can learn so much about a person just by observing him. Every human being exhibits clues to his background. Studying a person's body language will provide important information about his character.

Conduct and language

The conduct of a person can be traced to his upbringing. A well-mannered person will most often belong to a noble lineage. Those from underprivileged backgrounds may not be sophisticated in their demeanour simply because they don't know any better. The language a person speaks tells you about the region he comes from. In India, we have multiple languages and accents. It's easy to identify where a person is from based on these cues.

Affection and physique

A person's attitude towards you shows his level of affection for you. If he's warm and caring, he likes you. If he's rude and indifferent, he doesn't care for you. A person's love and respect for another human being determines how he treats the other person. If a person is strong and healthy, it means that he eats well and exercises regularly.

3.35

Pure is the water that is underground
Pure is that woman who is loyal to her husband
Pure is that king who is benevolent
And pure is that Brahmin who is content

Indian culture has always given importance to purity, both external and internal. Here, external purity refers to freedom from contamination. Internal purity refers to a high moral code. However, internal purity is something which cannot be seen but only experienced.

Pure water and pure woman

Underground water is considered the purest since it is devoid of any pollutants. Nowadays, as soon as it reaches rivers and lakes, it gets contaminated, thanks to the waste that is already in these bodies of water. According to Chanakya, a chaste woman is one who is loyal to her husband. She commands the respect of society.

Pure king and pure Brahmin

A king is pure if he is benevolent and takes care of his subjects as he does his own children. He makes their happiness his priority. A wise man is pure only when he is content. Dissatisfaction makes people commit immoral acts even if they are usually wise. A Brahmin is also fallible. Finally, inner purity matters the most.

3.36

Practice sustains learning
Good conduct sustains family ties
An *arya* is known by his goodness
And anger is seen in the eyes

In this verse Chanakya talks about how one can improve oneself
with the help of knowledge and good behaviour.

Learning and family ties

Practice is the very foundation of learning. One may have learnt to
play the flute, but if one does not practice it every day, the lessons
are lost.

The good conduct of each family member sustains a family. If the
members keep quarrelling with each other, the family unit will
break apart.

Arya and anger

How does one identify an *arya* (a noble person)? Chanakya says that
a noble person is known by his goodness. His acts and deeds make
him noble. When a person is angry, his eyes reflect the emotion. As
they say, eyes are the windows to the soul.

3.37

Goodness attained by a prudent person
Turns up fine
As a gem set in gold
Adds on shine

Everyone has certain qualities that stand out. Chanakya says that
in addition to good qualities, one needs to have a long-term plan to
succeed in the long run.

Goodness of a prudent person

A prudent person is one who carefully plans out his actions. He takes into account the impact of his actions on his every move. Such a person will be successful in all his endeavours in the long term.

Gem set in gold

A prudent person who is also good-natured is like a gem set in gold. Gold by itself is a precious metal. Yet a gem set within the gold increases the attractiveness of the gold. Similarly, noble values in an excellent thinker and planner add more value to that person.

3.38

**If the one who has wits is possessed by power
Where else can the dim-witted gain strength?
Remember the proud lion in the forest
A jackal drew him to his death!**

What is real power? It is the ability to think, says Chanakya. Those who are intelligent are the really powerful. Chanakya explains his observation with the example of a lion and jackal.

Who has the real power?

Merely sitting on a throne doesn't make someone a powerful king. A king's real clout is in his intelligence. He may lose his throne but his clever mind will always be with him. Using this mind, he can always plan to regain his throne. So is the case with ordinary people; if you're not smart, no one will respect you, no matter what post you hold in any organisation.

The lion and the jackal

Even a common person can gain the upper hand if he uses his intelligence. There is a story in the *Panchatantra* in which a lion is outwitted by a jackal. The lion is considered the king of the jungle. But this one was very proud and arrogant. Fed up being harassed, the jackal, the clever one, devised a cunning plan by which he pushed the lion to his death. So the mighty can also fall when the power of intellect comes into play.

3.39

What work is too heavy for the strong?
What place is too remote for the tradesmen?
Which country is alien to the learned?
Who can be rude to the soft-spoken?

Nothing can stop those who have their heart set on a goal. Not even the sky is the limit. Those who have tremendous willpower can achieve anything. Great men and women of high resolve have changed the course of the world and will continue to do so.

Workers and tradesmen

There is no work that is too heavy or difficult for a person who is able-bodied and strong. A capable person will find ways to get things done, even in the most impossible situations. Ambitious traders will reach any remote part of the world, take Vasco da Gama for example. Their thirst for new experiences and markets drive them to the distant corners of the earth.

The learned and the soft-spoken

Those who are learned are welcome in any country, because they bring their skills with them. So for such a person, no country is alien. For example, millions of Non-Resident Indians (NRIs) work in various sectors around the world. They are invited to work and live in other countries because of their superior skillsets; they add value to any country they go to. And nobody will behave rudely to a person who is pleasant and soft-spoken. An agreeable personality draws friends and acquaintances, not enemies.

3.40

What is a worst defect than greed?
What is a meaner act than betrayal?
If you are truthful, you don't need to do penance
If you have a clear conscience, you don't need to go
on pilgrimage
There is no greater distinction than goodness
If you are great, you don't need decoration
There is no better wealth than education
And ill fame is worse than death

Chanakya teaches us the finer points about greed, betrayal, truth, clear conscience, goodness, greatness, education and ill fame—all in a single verse.

Greed, betrayal, truth and clear conscience

According to Chanakya, greed is the worst defect one could have. If you betray someone who trusts you, it is the meanest act you can commit. There is no need for penance if you are truthful in everyday dealings. Many people embark on pilgrimages and visit numerous holy placed to purge their sins. However, if you have a clear conscience, there is no need for you to go on a pilgrimage.

Goodness, greatness, education and ill fame

If you are a good soul, why do you need a character certificate from others? Your goodness itself is your distinction. If you are a great person and you are aware of it, you do not need others to endorse you. Your character speaks for yourself. Education is the greatest wealth; it cannot be stolen or taken away from you. So never stop learning, even in your old age. And according to Chanakya, infamy is worse than death. Always protect your name by doing the best work you can.

3.41

**The king only speaks once
The pundit also speaks only once
A man marries off his daughter only once
All these three are done only once**

Certain things are done only once. One should know their importance and the fact that their repetition diminishes their value.

The king and pundit speaks only once

A king has supreme authority over his subjects. He gives an order only once and does not have to say it repeatedly. That is the power of command. And the wise Brahmin also has to say something for his followers to grasp the meaning. He is respected by all for the depth of his knowledge. What he teaches is to be grasped at once and he should not to be asked to repeat his words.

Wedding of the daughter

In Indian culture, the wedding of the daughter is the responsibility of her parents. In Hindu weddings, there is a *kanyadan* ritual, the symbolic giving away of one's daughter by her father. According to Chanakya, this act should be performed only once, thereby implying the seriousness and sanctity of marriage and family as an institution.

3.42

A Brahmin who is discontent
A king who is content
A modest courtesan
And an immodest homemaker
Are all doomed

Some roles and professions demand certain qualities. To excel in these roles, one needs to have those specific abilities. For example, a butcher can't be scared of blood and likewise a magician can't be too honest.

Downfall of Brahmins and kings

A Brahmin shouldn't be greedy. He is expected to live the life of a sage. He should be the one showing the right path to people, advising them against illegal and immoral practices. If he is discontent, his downfall begins. While on the other hand, a king should not be content. He should always be looking for ways to better the lives of his subjects. If he is content, then other ambitious kings will conquer his kingdom. To be continuously active should be the main priority of a king.

Downfall of prostitutes and wives

A shy prostitute will not be able to make ends meet. Though an unfortunate profession, her wages come from her patrons who seek her out for pleasure. If she is not able to entertain her patrons, she will lose her business. However, a wife or homemaker should not lead an immodest life. An indecent woman breaks up her family and stands to lose her loved ones.

3.43

**A man's speech should befit the occasion
His good deeds should match his capacity
His wrath should be in proportion to his power
One who knows these is a pundit indeed**

Understanding one's own positive and negative attributes will help a person succeed in life. In this *neeti*, Chanakya talks about some of those attributes to explain their importance in an intelligent man's life.

Speech and good deeds

According to Chanakya, one's speech should suit the occasion one is a part of. Be mindful of where you are and who you are with before stating what is on your mind. For example, it is indecorous to make jokes at a funeral. Maintain decorum when you are with colleagues or seniors. People lose respect quickly for those who behave crudely.

A person's good deeds should be measured as per his capacity. Never give away more than what you have. Also, don't be stingy. If you have the means to support someone in need, do so.

Wrath

Anger is a powerful tool. However, it can also get out of hand quickly. Keep in mind your standing in society and your clout before you unleash your wrath on someone. A rabbit cannot imitate a lion's roar. Never direct your anger at someone more powerful than you are; you will come to regret it. A person who understands all the above is a wise man, indeed. He will live a peaceful and fruitful life.

3.44

**Maybe no one advised Brahma, the creator,
To infuse fragrance in gold
To put fruits on sugarcane
To give flowers to the sandalwood tree
To bestow wealth on the scholar and
To grant long life to the king**

Certain things in the universe are how they are. They are part of nature's law. So let us accept them and face life's realities.

Gold, sugarcane and sandalwood tree

In this *neeti*, Chanakya talks about how Lord Brahma, the creator of the universe, overlooked certain aspects while crafting his masterpiece. Maybe no one advised him on these gaps. Imagine a world where gold smells good, sweet sugarcane bestows fruits and the sandalwood tree has equally fragrant flowers! It would have been lovely!

Scholar and king

Scholars are not business men; they don't sell knowledge for profit. Many of them lack the knack to make money; they don't prioritize money over knowledge. As a result, most learned men are not wealthy. Similarly, in the olden days a king did not live long since he was frequently on the battlefield. Kings belonged to the warrior clan and for warriors, death is always at the doorstep. Like wealth for a scholar, long-life for a king is very desirable. Change in reigns plunges a kingdom into confusion and chaos. It takes a long time before normality is restored. In the meantime, the subjects suffer the consequences. That's why a long-living king is ideal. But that is rarely the case. So one has to be happy with how life is, because this is how the creator intended it. Be content with what you have.

CHAPTER 4

LEARNING

4.1

**Parents are the enemies
Of a child who is not given education
He stands like a crane amidst swans
In any social gathering**

Education is the best gift parents can give their children. Chanakya says that those parents who don't send their kids to school are their kids' real enemies. These children stand to become misfits when they grow up.

Parents become enemies

One of the most important responsibilities of parents is to give their children the best schooling they can afford. Today, urban parents spend lakhs of rupees a year in school fees alone in order to provide their kids with a world-class education. Education is a child's birthright. Good education helps children prepare to face the world as adults. According to Chanakya, those parents who neglect their children's education are committing a crime and are failing their children.

A crane amidst swans

An illiterate person stands out like a crane among a group of swans in social gatherings. People view such a person as a misfit. Children are the future. No parent wants his child shunned by society. So help your child get the best training you can offer.

4.2

Though Sanskrit has refined my mind
I'm inclined to learn other languages
Just as gods yearn for the kisses of celestial nymphs
Even after consuming the *amrit*

We are never content with what we have. We keep asking for more. That is human nature. Chanakya gives here two examples to show that even after achieving the best, we crave for something more.

The Sanskrit language

Sanskrit is known to be one of India's most ancient and revered languages. It is said that the process of learning Sanskrit refines one's thinking. Sanskrit words produce vibrations of sound that resonate strongly. Yet, Chanakya says he is inclined to learn more languages. The more languages one knows, the more versatile one becomes. Such a person is sought after, both in the job scene and in social circles.

Nectar and celestial nymphs

The *puranas* narrate the story of gods and demons fighting for the nectar of immortality, the *amrit*. Even after consuming the nectar, the gods pined for the kisses of *apsaras*, the heavenly damsels. There is no end to desire. Even gods are not immune to it. Be mindful of the nature of your desire; it shouldn't land you in trouble at the end of the day.

4.3

A scholar is honoured everywhere
A scholar is respected by the people
Knowledge brings all gains
Knowledge is indeed honoured everywhere

In this verse, Chanakya shows his admiration for scholars and the knowledge they possess. Note that Chanakya himself was a great intellectual respected by all.

Scholars

Scholars are held in high regard in the world, both by kings and the common man. They are honoured with awards and titles too, over the ages. That is the respect scholars command.

Knowledge

Knowledge has no parallel, not even wealth. A learned man has all the wealth he needs within himself. He need not beg or steal; he can create wealth using his intelligence. Knowledge is valued around the world. Aim to be a scholar rather than a millionaire. Wealth doesn't guarantee respect (even a criminal can be rich) but knowledge certainly does.

4.4

A person who is blessed with beauty, Riches and a noble family background Is still worthless without education Like the kimshuka flower without fragrance

In this *neeti*, Chanakya reminds us again about the value of education. A person may have everything else but without education he is worthless.

Education

Who wouldn't like to be good-looking, affluent and have an illustrious family background? These three privileges can take a person far, but only if that person is well educated. Without education, all these blessings are useless. Nobody desires the company of an ignorant person, no matter how rich and handsome he is.

Flower without fragrance

Kimshuka is an attractive flower. But if you go near it once, you will discover that it does not have any fragrance at all. For this reason, you could even mistake it for an artificial flower. And suddenly, all the admiration you had for the flower disappears. Chanakya uses this analogy to make us understand that only external beauty is not enough. Strong character, which is essential for a good personality, develops only with education.

4.5

Of what use is a noble family
To men without education
A scholar even from a low family
Wins the gods' admiration

In this *neeti* Chanakya again brings up the point that without education everything else is useless.

Noble family without education

It is a great privilege to be born in a high-class family. A person belonging to a noble family will have name, fame and money to last a lifetime. However, if that person isn't educated, what is the use of such an illustrious background, asks Chanakya. He will not be able to function on his own; he will be dependent on those who are learned and therefore more intelligent than him. In effect, he will just be a puppet in the hands of those who are educated.

Scholar from a low family

Knowledge doesn't discriminate. Whether rich or poor, noble or common, anyone can learn, if given a chance and proper training. The gods admire scholars even if they are low-born, says Chanakya. A wise person garners everyone's respect.

4.6

Like a wish-granting cow (Kamadhenu)
Even in hard times knowledge bears fruit
While abroad, knowledge nurtures like a mother
Knowledge is like a hidden treasure

Knowledge has great value. However, many people still feel that knowledge doesn't do any good and education is a waste of time. Instead, they would rather let their children start work at a young age so they can provide additional income for the family. But the truth is that knowledge is like unused currency. It will come to a person's aid in the most difficult of times.

Knowledge as, the wish-granting cow

Kamadhenu is the name of the cow that resides in heaven. She is famous for fulfilling the wishes of gods. Here Chanakya compares knowledge to Kamadhenu, saying knowledge comes to the rescue of the learned during hardships. With the help of his intelligence, a scholar can bail himself out of the trickiest of situations.

Knowledge is like a mother

A mother never forsakes her child, whatever the situation the child is in. Similarly, knowledge nurtures its possessor like a mother; she is always there when needed. All the individual has to do is apply his intellect in times of need. Knowledge is also like hidden treasure. It is the only kind of wealth that cannot be stolen.

4.7

**The poor may not be wanting
But the rich want more, no doubt
In fact, without knowledge
One remains wanting more and more**

There is no end to human desire. A poor person may want very little as compared to a rich man, but everyone wants something or the other at all times. Knowledge is the only remedy for desire.

The wants of the poor and rich

The poor may only want their basic needs met, like housing, clothing and meals. However, the rich who are used to their luxuries wish for more opulence.

The power of knowledge

What will extinguish the wants of a person once and for all? Only the gems of knowledge, says Chanakya. Ignorance propels desire. The urge to compete with others in order to obtain materialistic things stems from ignorance. The one who is truly learned knows he needn't compete with anyone and is secure in his surroundings. So in short, in order to feel content, you have to expand your mind.

4.8

**A rogue will never attain goodness
Even if he is trained in many ways
And the neem tree will not become sweet
Even if soaked in milk and ghee**

The inherent nature of some things doesn't change at all. It's the same with certain people. Even if you try various means to reform them, their core will not change. Chanakya gives two examples here.

A rogue

An unprincipled and wicked man cannot become good even if someone trains him. He will always remain a rogue. According to Chanakya, his basic character will not change.

The *neem* tree

The *neem* tree has bitter leaves and bark. Can it be made sweet? No, not even if you keep it soaked in milk and honey. The *neem* will always taste bitter. Chanakya compares wicked people to the *neem* tree and says the essentials of both won't change, no matter how hard you try. It is better not to waste your efforts on such people.

4.9

**Even a guru who has taught you just a word
should be worshipped
He who does not worship a guru
Is born a dog for a hundred years
And then at last as a *Chandala***

Teachers command the greatest respect, for they impart wisdom, the mightiest of all gifts. Some teachers may teach you a number of subjects and yet others may teach you a skill or two outside the academic realm. Anybody who has taught you even a little bit should be given due respect or you may suffer the consequences, warns Chanakya.

A guru who has taught you just a word

Whether it is the professor who taught you molecular physics or your grandfather who showed you how to hook the bait on a fishing rod, both deserve reverence as teachers. Both taught you something of value. According to Chanakya, even a person who has taught you a single word should be worshipped as a guru. It is not necessary that all lessons involve long lectures or classrooms. Any person who knows a skill that can be imparted is a person of significance.

The life of a *Chandala*

According to Chanakya, the one who mistreats his guru will be born as a dog for hundred years. And after those hundred years, he will be born a *Chandala*, a dog-eater, the lowest rung in the social class ladder (during Chanakya's time) in *Sanatana Dharma*. Simply put, whoever disrespects his guru is doomed.

4.11

**No messenger can travel around the sky
No exchange of tidings comes from there
The voice of its inhabitants are not heard
And there is no contact with them
Therefore, a *Dvija* who can predict
The solar and lunar eclipses should be called a scholar**

There are some people who have superhuman powers. A *Dvija* is one of them, says Chanakya. He lists the reasons why a Brahmin should be considered a scholar.

No messenger from the sky

During Chanakya's time, it was unimaginable to have a messenger from the sky deliver news on celestial tidings. Today we have satellites to give us real-time updates on what's happening in space. In the olden days it was difficult for humans to gather any reliable information on stars and planets.

A true scholar

In ancient times, a *Dvija* calculated and predicted eclipses and other planetary events. Since Brahmins were the only ones with Vedic knowledge, they used Vedic mathematics to calculate the incidents of solar and lunar eclipses. People believed that eclipses were a bad omen and avoided cooking, eating and drinking water during this period. It was thought that one would suffer from food poisoning if one did so. It was therefore important to know when such eclipses occurred. A person who could calculate these incidences was considered a true scholar.

4.12

**Just as obtaining clear water
From the underground using a pick-axe
A diligent student obtains knowledge
From his teacher**

Acquiring knowledge is not easy. One needs to put in hard work in one's pursuit of knowledge. Chanakya compares the effort to digging for water underground.

Digging for water

In the olden days, people used pick-axes to dig wells. It was a very time-consuming activity. From dawn to dusk men excavated the earth's surface to find underground water. It was a slow and steady effort.

Knowledge

Chanakya compares the sweet underground water to knowledge, since both are precious and difficult to obtain. A good student has to be patient. He should persist in the face of adversities and be able to extract as much knowledge as possible from his teacher, bit by bit.

4.13

The scriptures are countless, knowledge is in abundance,
Time is short, many a hindrance
So choose your pick wisely
Like a swan drinking only milk from the milk-water mix

The world of knowledge is vast, abundant and ever-growing. But time is short and there's so much more to learn. So what does one do?

The world of knowledge

There are innumerable scriptures in every religion. With each generation, more books are published; there is more information on your fingertips, thanks to the internet. Knowledge in every field is expanding daily. But there's only so much time to imbibe information. How can one learn so much in so little time?

Extract the essence like a swan

Some people believe that swans can separate milk from water and drink only milk from the mix. One cannot learn everything. There's a limit to how much knowledge one can accumulate in one's short lifespan. It is better to choose wisely from the array of options available to you. Chanakya advises people to be like swans and focus only on the necessary and avoid the trivial.

4.14

Learn one virtue from a lion, one from a crane,
Four from a cock,
Five from a crow, six from a dog,
And three from a donkey

In the next couple of verses, Chanakya explains the qualities one
should learn from the various members of the animal kingdom.

4.15

Whatever work, big or small
A man intends to do must be done
Doing the same with full strength and wholeheartedness
Is a quality that can be learned from a lion

The lion is the king of the animal kingdom. He knows how to
command the entire jungle. Chanakya here gives the ultimate
formula for being a good leader.

What has to be done must be done

No work is too big or small to be accomplished. Don't assume a
casual approach towards your responsibilities. Instead, when you
commit to doing something, do it wholeheartedly. Do the work
with a focused mind and sharp intellect. The more attentive you
are, the better the output.

Give your full

Don't do anything half-heartedly. Put your entire being into your
work. In this way, you will inspire those around you. This kind of

focus, intensity and strength, as symbolized by the lion, makes a person a good leader.

4.16

A wise man should restrain
His senses like a crane
And accomplish his goals after
The due inspection of the place, time and ability

If you want to be wise, you should first know your strengths and weaknesses. Start on a goal only after a careful review of the goal and yourself.

Senses under control

A wise man is one who keeps his senses under control, like a crane. A crane can stand still for hours waiting for its prey, fish. Such a focused mind is essential for producing great results.

Evaluate everything

Before undertaking any activity, you should asses its pros and cons. These include the appropriate place and time, and also your own abilities. This will help minimize any obstacles that could appear while executing a particular activity.

4.17

To wake up early,
To take a bold stand in a fight,
To share anything evenly with the relatives,
And to own one's own bread through hard work
Are the things one can learn from a rooster

Here Chanakya tells us what to learn from a rooster. There are four qualities mentioned in his observation.

Rising early; taking a bold stand

We know that the early bird gets the worm and so the rooster must be a clever one since he wakes up first and rouses the others. He is also unafraid to fight for what he wants. Have you ever seen a cockfight? Another impressive quality of the rooster is that he doesn't bow down to anyone easily and stands his ground.

Sharing and self-earning

Observe a rooster with his family. He struts around searching for food and when he gets a worm, he divides it equally with all his family members. He isn't greedy or selfish. Also, he fends for himself and doesn't depend on others to bring him food.

4.18

Making love in private, Boldness, storing away useful items, Watchfulness and not trusting anyone easily, These five qualities have to be learned from the crow

The crow is not liked very much. It is not beautiful to look at. However, there are five qualities one can learn from this creature.

Protecting one's privacy, boldness and storing things away

You will never catch a crow mating in public; it is as if the bird understands and respects the sanctity of intimacy. One should be bold in one's outlook and not worry about what others think. No matter how many times a crow is shooed away, it returns and waits for an opportunity to steal a morsel of food. A crow is also clever in storing away bits and bobs for later use.

Watchfulness and non-trusting attitude

A crow is extremely watchful. Haven't you noticed how a crow scans its surroundings, turning its head this way and that? Being alert keeps the crow from getting harmed by humans and other birds of prey. Observation is a good administrative quality. In addition, a crow does not trust others easily. Better safe than sorry, seems to be his motto.

4.19

A glutton but content with small (portions of food),
Deep sleeper but is awake at short call,
Faithful to the master and bold,
Take six virtues from the dog's fold

We can learn six qualities from the dog, a faithful animal.

A glutton but content

A dog is fond of eating. On one hand, he is greedy and enjoys food, but on the other hand he is happy with what you give him. One should learn from a dog in matters of life—aspire for more yet be happy with what one has.

Quick, faithful and bold

Another characteristic of a dog is that he can get deep sleep immediately. However, he is also extremely alert and can be up and about in a second if anything disturbs him. He is also faithful to his master and ever ready to protect him.

4.20

Though tired, a donkey carries his load
Indifferent to heat and cold,
Grazes always with ease
Learn from the donkey these three qualities

A donkey is usually considered a dim-witted animal. However, Chanakya sees and learns from everybody. Here he explains three qualities of a donkey.

Tired but still works

A donkey is a beast of burden and carries heavy loads on its back. After travelling some distance, this load is sure to cause some unease to the donkey. But the donkey does not stop. It doesn't matter if the weather is hot or cold, a donkey carries on with its work. Similarly, even if one is tired, one should not stop till one's work is done.

Indifferent

A donkey is indifferent to his circumstances. He does not panic under pressure. Endurance is also a great quality which enables him to face all situations with equanimity. He doesn't bother about what he eats. He grazes on whatever is available to him.

4.21

Whoever practices these
Twenty virtues
Will be invincible
In any situation

According to Chanakya, if a person practices the 20 virtues of all the birds and animals described in the above verses, he will become invincible.

Twenty virtues

Observe the animals and birds listed in the above verses carefully and understand their virtues. They use their specific qualities to survive effectively in the brutal animal world.

Become invincible

If one imbibes all these qualities, one will become unbeatable and
all-powerful. By adopting these 20 qualities, you can become a
winner in life.

CHAPTER 5

WEALTH

5.1

It's better to live under a tree in a forest,
Where tigers and elephants hunt,
With leaves, fruits and water for nourishment,
A bed of grass to sleep,
The tree bark for a dress,
Than to live without money
In the midst of kith and kin

Where there is money, there is respect. Even your own relatives will not respect you if you are poor. It is better to leave your family home and live in the forest than face the insults of your relatives, suggests Chanakya.

Living in a forest

Chanakya is a practical philosopher. Living in a forest where wild animals roam and where one has only fruits and berries to eat, grass to sleep on and tree bark to clothe oneself with may sound harsh. However, but it is better than some other options, as Chanakya cleverly points out.

Insults of kith and kin

Being a forest dweller is better than living in the midst of relatives who are cruel to you just because you are poor. Those family members who do not contribute financially to the running of a family are not respected at all. Harsh but true. They are also insulted to a large extent, either directly or indirectly by their own folk. It is better to preserve one's dignity and live amongst animals than endure such family members.

5.2

A man who loses money is deserted by friends,
By his wife, well-wishers and dependents
On his becoming rich, they hang on to him again
In this world money is indeed a true ally of man!

Who is man's real friend? Money, says Chanakya. It is indeed a bold statement. He goes on to explain the reasons.

Deserted by friends, spouse, well-wishers and dependents

In this materialistic world, a person who is not financial stable is quickly discarded by his friends; he is deemed worthless. His own wife leaves him. His well-wishers also give up on him. Those who are dependent on him, like his children and parents, also abandon him.

On becoming rich again

Interestingly, when he regains his wealth, he regains respect from the same people who turned their backs on him when he was penniless. His friends and relatives rebuild their relations with him. So strange is the nature of money. This is a hard reality of life, says Chanakya.

5.3

Where fools are not adored
Food grains are properly stored
Husband and wife do not clash
There Lakshmi comes on her own accord

Lakshmi is the goddess of wealth. When does she appear?

Where fools are not adored and food grains are stored properly

Lakshmi resides where scholars are revered, not fools. Knowledge is the gateway to prosperity. If you are intelligent, you know how to manage your money. Fools don't respect money, and therefore don't respect the goddess of wealth.

Well-maintained granaries ensure that food is available at all times. Where people are well-nourished, the goddess of wealth automatically stays.

Where there is marital harmony

For a husband and wife to have a difference of opinion is normal. But, a disagreement should not lead to a full-fledged fight. A house where spouses live in harmony attracts prosperity because the couple's energy is not wasted on unnecessary quarrels. Their calm and productive thinking leads to the accumulation of wealth.

5.4

**He who wears unwashed clothes, has dirty teeth,
Is a glutton, speaks rudely,
Sleeps even after sunrise,
Will lose Lakshmi's favour**

There are ways to attract Lakshmi, and others to repel her. Chanakya describes the people who stand to lose the goddess's favour.

Unwashed clothes, dirty teeth, rude speech

External cleanliness is very important in addition to inner purity. If you have poor personal hygiene or speak crudely, you will be disliked by all around you, not to mention Lakshmi herself.

Sleeping after sunrise

You may have heard from your grandmother that sleeping past after the sunrise is bad for you. Well, Chanakya is of the same opinion. He warns us that a lazy attitude in the morning will drive away goddess Lakshmi. Early morning is the best time to organize one's day without any disturbances and get an early start. Remember, the early bird gets the worm. So wake up early and get ahead in life.

5.5

Unjustly earned money
May stay for ten years
In the eleventh year
Along with the principal it disappears

Many think that money can be earned by hook or by crook. Chanakya warns us about unethical methods of earning money. Money earned sinfully will disappear sooner or later, making one poorer than before.

Unjustly earned money

Today, society seems not to care how money is earned. However, Chanakya says that money earned through illegitimate means is dirty money. Don't glorify such wealth; it will not stay forever.

Only for a decade

Wealth earned through illegal means may stay with you for 10 years, but in the 11th year both the principal and interest will disappear, warns Chanakya. It is better to earn money through ethical means over the long term rather than unethically for the short term.

5.6

**Let me not have the wealth
That is the result of a fight
Or attained through illegal means**

There is good wealth and bad wealth. And Chanakya, through this *neeti*, is offering a prayer to attract only the good kind.

Wealth acquired wrongfully

Earn wealth only through rightful means. Riches procured through *adharmic* or immoral means will not be of any help to you; it will only attract trouble.

Better to not have such wealth

Chanakya is praying that one should not be blessed with the wrong kind of wealth. Such wealth does not have any merit. Wrongfully acquired wealth is impermanent and will only cause you trouble. Living in constant fear of the law is no way to live, even if you are the richest man on earth.

5.7

**A straw is light, cotton is lighter than straw,
A beggar is the lightest of all;
Why doesn't the wind blow him away?
Because it fears he will ask for alms!**

In this verse, Chanakya is revealing some disturbing truths about poverty. Apparently not even the wind wants to touch a pauper.

A beggar is lighter than cotton

A straw is very light in weight. Compared to a straw, cotton is even lighter. But a beggar is lighter than even cotton because he is malnourished and he has nothing in his pocket. So it is possible for a gust of wind to blow him away. But we don't see that happening. Why?

Even the wind discards the poor

The poor are a liability, even to Mother Nature, it seems. Chanakya's dark humour is apparent in this *neeti*. He explains that the wind does not carry away a beggar despite his lightness because even the wind is scared that the beggar will demand alms from it. Here Chanakya is trying to highlight the issues of poverty. Nobody wants to be responsible for a poor person. On the other hand, money brings friends and family closer. It is sad but true. So guard your wealth with all you have. You don't want to end up like the beggar in this example.

5.8

One should save money for the rainy day
Do not say, "Do the rich have calamities anyway?"
For Lakshmi is *chanchala*, when she walks out
Accumulated wealth also goes away!

Life is a mix of good and bad times. Therefore, one should be prepared for bad times. Save money, advises Chanakya. Even the rich should not take their wealth for granted.

Rainy days

Rainy days are symbolic of the time when earning opportunities are sparse and money is hard to come by. How do you plan to sustain your family during such times? Don't fool yourself by thinking that bad times won't come your way. It is wise to save every penny you can today. Time and tide wait for no one, remember that.

Calamities can affect even the rich

The rich are not insulated from calamities and bad luck. The reason for this is the *chanchala* (fickle) nature of goddess Lakshmi. She keeps moving from place to place and people to people. When she decides to walk away, your accumulated wealth may also go down the drain. Therefore, save money and pray for your good fortune to last.

5.9

Of what use is that wealth
Which is either like a monogamous bride,
Or is like a woman of the streets
Enjoyed even by the wayfarers

The behaviour of wealth is strange. It cannot be with one person. However, being easily available diminishes its value. Chanakya forces us to think about the real nature of wealth using this verse. He uses the examples of a monogamous bride and a prostitute, reflecting the thinking of his time.

A monogamous bride

A monogamous bride is one who is committed to her husband wholeheartedly; she does not indulge in any extra-marital affairs. Take the case of wealthy people who hoard their wealth and don't share it. In this sense, their money is like a monogamous bride. The money neither goes out of their grips not is it helpful to anyone else.

Woman of the streets

On the other extreme is the woman of the streets, a prostitute. She does not hesitate to sleep with anyone, including travellers passing by. So here Chanakya stresses the point that wealth that is exchanged freely is not ideal either; such wealth is not to be trusted. With these two extreme examples, Chanakya asks a weighty question, "Does one really understand the nature of wealth?"

5.10

**What a wonder it is
The doings of the great are strange
They treat wealth as light as a straw
But when they obtain it, how they bend under its weight!**

The power of money is enormous. Even great people become subservient to it. Even though they may deny it, they do change after becoming wealthy.

Treating wealth lightly

Great people are revered for their deeds and not for their wealth. Many of them rebuff wealth. Some of them even consider wealth to be as inconsequential as a straw. However, something strange happens when they acquire wealth.

Under the weight of money

The same great minds who once denounced money submit to its influence, once they prosper. They come under the sway of wealth. They protect their newfound wealth and want more of it. Chanakya explains that no one escapes the charm of money. Indeed, money rules the world.

5.11

**A rich man attracts friends
Kin also turn to the moneyed
The wealthy one alone is called a man
The affluent alone are considered wise**

The practical philosopher that Chanakya was, here reveals some more profound thoughts on the nature of wealth.

Friends and relatives flock to the rich

A person who is well to do attracts a lot of friends. You may have been lonely all your life but notice how many "friends" you suddenly make when you've made a name for yourself and become rich. So is the case with relatives. They too tend to stick to those family members who are wealthy.

Wealthy is considered wise

This may sound strange, but those who are wealthy are considered wise by others. Indeed, the one who has wealth in this world is also respected and adored. He considered to be the perfect man—a person whose achievements and successes are celebrated.

5.12

**Distribution of accumulated wealth
Provides the safety net
Just as incoming fresh water
Is saved by letting out stagnant water**

Spending your savings is not a wise move, says Chanakya. It doesn't serve the purpose of providing a safety net for you and your family in difficult times. Guard your savings as you would protect a newborn; let it grow and give you return on your investment.

Distribution of accumulated wealth

Chanakya is using his wit to hit home his point about the importance of savings in this *neeti*. He is comparing spending one's savings to preserving fresh water by letting out stagnant water. It's crucial to start saving money at a young age. Many youngsters and some old timers spend their savings on unnecessary luxury items without leaving some of their earnings for a rainy day. This is a dangerous habit; money should not be wasted. A person without money is as good as dead.

Fresh water and stagnant water

How can incoming fresh water be saved by letting our stagnant water? Both will be equally polluted in the end. So no one benefits by spending all of one's savings. Money is good only when it is in your pocket, so keep a strong grip on it.

5.13

One who compassionately gives a little
To a *Vipra* who is in distress is compensated abundantly
Hence, O king, what is given to a good *Vipra* is returned
Not in the same measure, but in an infinitely higher degree

This advice by Chanakya applies to the king and the common man alike. Here he describes the appropriate attitude to adopt when helping others.

Donate with compassion and respect

Do not help out of arrogance and the ego. Offer others whatever help you can provide from the goodness of your heart. Helping a distressed wise man, *Vipra*, will only strengthen your karma. Your contribution will be returned to you manifold. Therefore, even a small donation should be made with reverence.

Rewards of compassionate donation

Whatever you donate will be returned to you in abundance. However, do not expect anything in return while doing charity. Remember that your reward may not be up to you to choose; it will be decided by the universe.

5.14

O wise man, wealth should be given only to the virtuous
Never to anybody else
Same as water from the ocean
Vapoured into clouds turns sweet in between
Meets all living and nonliving beings' need
On the whole circle of earth indeed
Look! The same water ever so many cycles it turns
And back to the ocean it flows

Everyone wants wealth. But only the virtuous should get wealthy. Chanakya explains this idea using the analogy of water, clouds and the ocean.

Give wealth only to the virtuous

Give money only to those who deserve it. Those who deserve it are people of high moral standards. The undeserving will misuse the money. Only when the virtuous have the wealth is it used for good and reaches the needy. These noble investments multiply and return to the virtuous. This way, the cycle of wealth continues and helps people along the way.

Water from the ocean

The water in the ocean is limitless, but it is salty and cannot be consumed. However, when it evaporates, forms clouds and eventually becomes rain, the same salty water turns sweet and drinkable. Every living being needs water for survival. These clouds reach all living beings in the form of rain. With the help of water the earth flourishes. Finally, the same rain water flows back to the ocean, thus completing the cycle.

5.15

**Distribute your wealth, O kind hearted!
It shouldn't be hoarded
The great kings Karna, Bali and Vikramaditya
Attained their fame through charity
Just see the lament of the honeybees
who have lost their honey
They neither enjoyed the stored-up honey
nor did they give it in charity
And now someone else has taken it from them**

Give, give and give—this is the advice of the wise. Chanakya in the concluding verse of this section on wealth asks what the use of accumulating wealth is? It will be anyway taken away from you...

Distribute wealth

Start distributing your wealth now, says Chanakya. Be kind like the great men of yore, like Karna, Bali and Vikramaditya. These three kings were great philanthropists and even today are revered for their generosity. They did not hoard their wealth. They used it to help the needy. It is because of their kindness that their fame remains intact.

Do not hoard wealth

Growing your savings is essential but hoarding wealth is not advisable. Just look at the honeybees. They collect honey from everywhere but don't enjoy it themselves or give it away in charity. They amass their sweet honey till someone comes and takes it away. What is the point of lamenting afterwards? In the same manner, we will lose all the wealth we have gathered once we die. Nobody carries their riches with them when they pass on. One doesn't get salvation nor gratification from hoarded wealth. Therefore, share your wealth as much as possible. At least you will accumulate some good karma.

CHAPTER 6

―――

INTERPERSONAL RELATIONS

6.1

Men who are successful in this world are those
Who are generous to one's own people,
Kind to attendants,
Smart with the malevolent,
Loving towards the good, shrewd with the wicked,
Frank with scholars,
Courageous with enemies, humble with the elderly,
And stern with women

How can one become successful in life? One has to deal with different types of people and deal with each of them differently. In this *neeti*, Chanakya gives guidelines to interact with a variety of people that will come your way.

Generosity, kindness, smartness, love and shrewdness

Be generous to your relatives and take care of them. You should be compassionate to your servants and helpers. With malicious people, it's better to counter them at their game. Be smart while dealing with them. Be loving towards those who are good to you. With those who make mischief, you should be firm.

Frankness, courage, humility and sternness

When it comes to dealing with scholars, it is better to be straightforward, because they are intelligent and can see through the drivel. Be courageous while dealing with your enemies. With the elderly, you should be humble for they have seen more of life. Women were considered inferior to men (both physically and mentally) during Chanakya's time, so he says while dealing with women, one must be stern, as if one is dealing with a naughty child. According to Chanakya, a person who has mastered the art of handling every type of personality is sure to succeed in this world.

6.2

He who considers another's wife as his mother
Another's money as a lump of clay
Pains and pleasures of all beings as his own
Is a true pundit

How should you treat others? What should your attitude be towards other human beings? Here Chanakya lists the appropriate way to perceive people and things that don't belong to you.

Another's wife and money

Always regard another man's wife as your own mother. In this way, you are showing respect for the woman, her husband and their relationship. This will help you garner the goodwill of that entire family and society in general. Money that does not belong to you should be treated as inconsequential. You should only enjoy the fruits you have earned through your hard work.

Pain and pleasures

One should be able to treat all beings as you do yourself. Try to see yourself in others; treat their pains and pleasures as your own. You are then at a higher level of spirituality. According to Chanakya, a person who knows this and also puts this wisdom to practice is indeed a pundit.

6.3

The one who criticizes others
Without knowing their merits
Is like the *Bhil* woman who discards
The pearl from the head of the elephant and
picks up the berry

One should be able to differentiate between good and bad. Only then will one be considered wise.

Criticizing others

Some of us like to criticize others at the drop of a hat, even if they are strangers. No wonder such a person lacks the ability to discern right from wrong, which is essential to succeed in life. Understand people well before judging them. You may not know what kind of difficulties they are experiencing in their life.

Bhil woman and berries

Chanakya compares a person who speaks ill about a stranger to an ill-informed *Bhil* woman (*Bhils* are a tribal hunting community of Rajasthan) who discards a pearl from the head of a dead elephant and collects berries from the forests instead. What a loss!

6.4

From the earth, on both hands,
Easily you lifted the mountain
That's why on earth and in heaven
Forever thy name became Giridhar
"Though in my heart I bear you
O triple-world sustainer! Does it matter?
O Keshav! What use is talking much!
By good work only one gets honoured!"

Here's an analogy about Krishna, also known as Giridhar, the one who holds up the mountain. For someone who has accomplished a lot, words are inconsequential.

Giridhar

The *Mahabharata* and *Srimad Bhagavatam* narrate the *leelas* of Lord Krishna. In one such story, Indra was upset because he was not worshipped in Krishna's village. Indra, in his anger, caused a heavy downpour. To protect his people, Krishna lifted the Govardhan mountain and gathered his whole village under it.

Honour

This act of Lord Krishna made him famous. People in the surrounding villages learned about his strength and glory. Now, does a person like Lord Krishna need to talk about himself? Good work will be honoured indeed. Let your work speak for itself.

6.5

**They alone are sons who are devoted to their father
He is a father who nurtures his children
A friend is the one who is a repository of faith
A wife is she in whom the husband finds satisfaction**

What are the roles and responsibilities of relatives and friends?
Chanakya here lists the duties of a son, father, friend and wife.

Sons and fathers

Good sons are those who are devoted to their fathers. Children are
expected to obey and respect their parents. An ideal father nurtures
his children; he educates them and brings them up with love, care
and discipline.

Friends and wives

A friend is one on whom you have complete faith, under any
circumstance. What use is a friend you cannot trust? Likewise, a
good wife is the one who loves and cares for her husband and family,
creating a happy and peaceful home.

6.6

**Fish, turtles and birds
Bring up their little ones
By means of attendance, attention and caress
And saintly men do the same with their associates**

How do you become a good parent and nurture your young ones?
Chanakya takes the examples of fish, turtles and birds to show you
how.

Nurturing young ones

Chanakya lists three ways in which one can raise children — keeping an eye on them, giving them your full attention and showering them with affection. Keep a close watch on your children so they don't end up in danger. Be attentive to their needs and support them in all ways you can. Lastly, a gentle caress can convey love and affection in a way a thousand words cannot. Watch how fish, turtles and birds look after their young ones and you will notice that they use these three ways effectively.

Saintly men and their associates

Respected men take care of their aides just as a parent cares for his child. A great mentor is someone who unselfishly nurtures his charge and helps him develop.

So be in the company of good people; you will always feel wanted and will have numerous opportunities to flourish.

6.7

Consider these five as your father:
The one who gave you birth,
The one who initiated you,
The one who taught you,
The one who provided for you,
And the one who protected you from fear

In this *neeti*, Chanakya talks about the five duties of a father. Anybody who has fulfilled any one of these duties should be considered a father figure.

Procreator, initiator and teacher

The man who is responsible for your birth automatically becomes your birth father. Similarly, the one who initiates you into a society, for example via the thread ceremony performed for Brahmin boys, also attains the status of a guardian in your life. Your guru should also be considered a paternal figure, because he imparts wisdom just as a father does to his child.

Provider and protector

Another duty of a father is to provide food, clothing and shelter to his family. He is the primary breadwinner. He has to ensure all his children are fed well even if he has not eaten. Anybody other than one's biological father who provides for one should also be respected as a father. A father also protects his children from fears and comforts them in their hour of need. If you have anyone in your life who helps you overcome your fears, he deserves to be revered as a father figure.

6.8

**The wife of the ruler, of the friend,
Of the preceptor,
Your wife's mother and your own mother,
All these five should be considered as mothers**

Who is a mother? Only the one who gave birth to you? Not according to Chanakya. According to this *neeti*, there are many important women in our lives whom we should respect as mothers.

Wife of the ruler, friend and preceptor

The wives of your king, friend and teacher should be considered as your mothers. They should be given due consideration and treated with respect.

Wife's mother and one's own mother

All mothers deserve love and respect. Even one's mother-in-law should be treated as one's own mother. Your own mother should also be looked after well. Instead of admitting her in an old-age home at the end of her life, care for her and comfort her, as she did for you when you were little. Don't forget your mother in your mindless pursuit of "finer things".

6.9

Fondle the child for five years
For the next ten, teach him discipline
Treat him as a friend
On his sixteenth year onwards

This is one of Chanakya's most well-known *neetis* on parenting. It is an age-old formula for good parenting.

The first five years and the next 10 years

A son should be fondled and pampered till he is five years old. A small child needs to be showered with love. During the next 10 years, i.e., from 5 to 15, he should be disciplined. Use a stick if necessary. These are crucial years during which a child's intelligence and character develop. Teach your child the value of discipline to help him flourish in the future.

Treat your child as your friend

After your child reaches 15 years of age, treat your him as your friend. Age 16 onwards, your parenting role is almost done. From then on, children require only your guidance and support. Give them freedom and also learn from them, the way friends learn from each other.

6.10

Avoid contact with the wicked
Choose the company of good people
Perform good deeds day and night
Remember always that life is ephemeral

Life is short, don't forget that. Make the best use of it. What use is regretting things that you could have done better?

Wicked and good people

Chanakya advises us to avoid evil-minded people. They can ruin your life with their negative influence. Therefore, choose the company of noble people. This will help you cultivate a positive outlook and thereby transform your life for good.

Always do good

When we die, we carry nothing with us—no wealth, titles or company. It is only the merits that we have earned, *punya*, that we carry along to the next life. Our karmic wealth is our true wealth. So perform many good deeds as you can. You never know when death will come calling. After all, life on earth is temporary.

6.11

The wise may marry a girl born to a respectable family
Even if she is not pretty
But do not marry a pretty girl from an undignified family
Alliance between families of equal status is preferable

Compatibility is crucial in every relationship. If two people are not compatible, no liaison will last long, especially in the case of marriage.

Pick plain above pretty

The decision to marry is an important one. It can make or break one's life. So choose your partner carefully, says Chanakya. It is wiser to marry someone who is well-bred and from a respectable family, versus an attractive person from a disrespectful family.

Match between equals

Avoid choosing an attractive spouse if he or she belongs to a family with poor values. Having a partner from a poor family is better than one belonging to a family devoid of morals. So choose an alliance with a family whose values are compatible with yours. Don't marry for beauty alone.

6.12

Social affairs, healthy fear,
Shame, kindness and liberality
Where these five are not found
Stay away from that society

A society will have a mix of both good and bad values. These values have an influence on its members. A society with more bad values than good will breed morally corrupt citizens.

Five qualities of a good society

Chanakya points out five qualities that make a good society. On the top of the list is social interaction—a society where people regularly meet and help each other will strengthen the bonds between people and promote welfare within the society. Second comes healthy fear—a place which upholds a constitution. This will make sure people live in a lawful society. Third is shame—a society devoid of shame is doomed; misconduct rules such a place. There will only be perpetual chaos. Fourth comes kindness—a place where no one is kind is no place to live and raise a family. Kindness is one of the marvelous qualities humans possess; without it, we are as good as animals. Fifth is the virtue of liberality—being open towards others' views is an essential mindset to live in harmony in a world full of people from varied cultures and backgrounds.

Stay away

If the above five qualities are not found in a society, it is not an ideal one to live in. Stay away, warns Chanakya, because such a society will breed criminals. And the danger is, living among them, you will become one of them.

6.13

**Avoid the person who is sweet in front of you
But tries to harm you behind your back
Because he is like a pot of poison
With milk on top**

Some people are excellent actors; they talk sweetly in front of you and when you turn your back, they won't hesitate a second to feed you to the sharks if they could. Beware of such people.

Sweet talkers

Certain people tend to mask their real feelings by indulging in sweet talks. They ooze charm and are extremely friendly. However, they don't mean what they say. Such double-faced, deceitful people are never to be trusted.

Keep off a phony

If you ever come across such a person, keep your distance. One shouldn't have a relationship with a person who is two-faced. He will deceive you. Such a person is like a pot of poisoned milk; it looks nutritious but is deadly.

6.14

**In sickness, suffering,
Famine and danger
At the king's gate and on the funeral ground
One who lends support is a real well-wisher**

Who is a real friend? The one who takes care of you during your time of need. Chanakya describes here the circumstances under which we discern who our real friends are.

Sickness, suffering and famine

When we are sick, we do not just need medicine but also the warmth and care of our friends to help us overcome our sickness. When we are going through bad times, we need people to help us to triumph over difficulties and to provide us with a support system. When we don't have access to adequate food, we need someone who can provide us meals. Those who are available to us during these times are real friends.

At the king's gate and at the funeral ground

Meeting a king is a joyous occasion; it shows that you have arrived. Only a few get a chance to meet important dignitaries and the joy of such rare occasions could be doubled if one has a friend to share it with. Of course, no one wants to die alone. If there is no one to mourn our death, what is the point of living? As bestselling author Robin Sharma famously asked, who will cry when you die? Real friends are those who are present at your funeral and mourn your passing.

6.15

**It's better to give up
Than to live in disgrace
The pain of death is only momentary
But the pain of disgrace lingers every day**

Living with humiliation is worse than death. Why suffer such shame? Death is better than disgrace. Chanakya is not advocating suicide here but merely reminding us to strive to live an honourable life.

Life and bad reputation

A person with credibility is respected in society while a person with a bad reputation is always ridiculed. If one is among the latter, it is better to leave that particular society than to face humiliation.

Temporary pain

When you give up something, you will no doubt be pained. However, it is better to endure temporary pain than to suffer forever. Disgrace is one such permanent pain. Why continue to live in shame, asks Chanakya.

6.16

The lower class wants wealth
The middle class wants both wealth and respect
But nobles want dignity alone
For dignity is the true wealth of men of honour

Different people have different desires. Their desires reflect the
class they belong to.

Lower and middle class people

Poor people want money because that's what is missing from
their lives. Since even their basic needs are not met, money is the
ultimate answer to all their problems. The middle class is different.
It knows the importance of honour. Since its basic needs are met,
it aspires for more. So it wishes for two things—money and respect.

Noble men and honour

Honour matters most to those in affluent families. They understand
that money cannot buy respect. Such people consider dignity their
real wealth, and don't compromise it. People always long for what
they don't have or what they can't get.

6.17

Praised by others
Even an unworthy person acquires merit
But falls short even Indra
If he blows his own trumpet

What is the yardstick of success? It is praise from others. However,
can one praise oneself and attain greatness? Chanakya addresses
this dilemma here.

Praise to the unworthy

When someone unworthy is praised by others, he gains some merit. The person looks worthy of the accolades he's getting even though he doesn't deserve them. This is not real fame. There is no substance to it. It's temporary. Real fame stands the test of time. Real fame sticks; time cannot erase it.

Blowing one's own trumpet

But if a person blows his own trumpet, he will lose recognition, no matter how worthy he is. Chanakya says even Indra, the god of gods, would also not be respected, if he praised himself. Others must praise you for the work you have done. Only then will you be held in high esteem.

6.18

**A Brahmin is happy with a good meal
A peacock is happy when thunder rumbles
A pious person is happy at others' prosperity
The wicked are happy when others are in trouble**

Everyone has a different source for their happiness. This realisation makes happiness a relative concept. Here Chanakya gives us four examples of how diverse people become happy based on their circumstances and situations.

The Brahmin and the peacock

The wise man is happy when he is served a good meal. For such men just food served with love is all that is required. The peacock is happy when the skies rumble in the anticipation of the rains. It dances with joy, fanning its feathers, to welcome the downpour.

The pious and the wicked

Pious men find their happiness in the happiness of others. They are
not jealous of others' success. On the other hand, the malicious are
happy when others are in trouble. They are sadists. They find joy
in hearing about others' calamities.

6.19

Gods, sages and parents
Are easily pleased
Relatives can be pleased with good hospitality
And pundits with a chance to deliver a discourse

Sometimes pleasing people requires great effort. However, things
can go smoothly if you know what they like, or what they expect.
Chanakya gives some tips on these matters in his unique way.

Gods, sages and parents

According to Chanakya, gods, sages and one's own parents are very
easily pleased; this could be because of the goodness of their hearts.
Even though they can be easily upset, they are the first to forgive.
They are large-hearted and kind.

Relatives and pundits

Kinsfolk are happy when you take care of them well. With the spirit
of hospitality, bring them together and give them love and respect.
What else do relatives want but to be served well? The pundit or the
scholar will be pleased with an opportunity to talk on the scriptures.
He will be pleased with you, if you organize such a lecture for him.

6.20

Test a servant when he is discharging his duties
Relatives during an adversity
Friends during an emergency
And a wife during misfortune

How can one assess a person's worth? When he is tested during difficult situations, is the answer. Gold is tested in fire. So, we too should test people's mettle in difficult situations to know how good they really are.

Servants and kinsfolk

To test the worth of a servant, observe how he accomplishes a difficult chore. What's his attitude towards his work? Is he honest and sincere? If he is enthusiastic and earnest, he can be trusted with any chore. It is the same case with relatives. Good relatives stick with you when you are going through a difficult time and offer their support.

Friends and wife

A friend in need is a friend indeed. Those who come to your rescue during an emergency are true friends. You will know whether your wife is committed to you when you face misfortune. If she still sticks with you through it all, she is a good wife. What use is a wife if she is with you only during the good times? It's when things go bad that your spouse should support you wholeheartedly.

6.21

Indulgence only spoils
Strictness is for the best
Therefore, with son and student
One should be strict, not indulgent

Whom do you prefer: a person who says yes to you or the one that says no? It is human tendency to not like people who disagree with you. Here Chanakya says it's better to be strict than overindulgent, especially with youngsters.

Indulgence and strictness

When one indulges in self-gratification, it is very harmful. To indulge is wrong, warns Chanakya. However, being strict is good, he adds, as it saves one from harm. Those who protect someone from harm are really good people indeed.

Son and student

One should be strict with children. Those who discipline their children are good parents. To love and discipline children simultaneously is the duty of a parent. So is the case with a student. A teacher should be strict with his disciple and lead him to greatness by helping develop his skills and aptitude.

6.22

**Whom one desires to harm
One should always speak endearingly
As a hunter intending to kill a deer
Sings to it melodiously**

Chanakya was renowned for his war strategies. He was a master in identifying the weakness of his enemy and annihilating him at an opportune time. In this particular *neeti*, Chanakya is doling out advice to triumph over one's adversaries.

Endearing words

Chanakya's tip on how to win over the enemy: speak to them lovingly. Please note that he is not advising you to be unethical, but helping you to strategize how to win over your enemy using the technique of sweet talk.

A hunter sings melodiously to his prey

Some deer hunters use melodious sounds to attract their prey. The deer, enchanted by the sweet melody, comes close to the hunter and keeps still. The hunter is then able to shoot the deer easily. In other words, it is better to seduce the enemy than to fight him directly. Use your brains instead of weapons to win over those who are against you.

6.23

Too much closeness to the king,
Fire, a religious preceptor and women are harmful
To be indifferent to them is not beneficial either
It is best to deal with them from a safe distance

It's best to keep a safe distance from certain people. Being too close is harmful but indifference is not useful either. The best way to deal with such people is by maintaining a distance.

Too much closeness is harmful

With respect to a king, fire, a religious teacher and women, overfamiliarity is dangerous. All the above are temperamental and dangerous when spurned. A king can have you executed if he's displeased; fire can burn you to cinders; a religious teacher can discredit you in society and women can ruin your reputation.

Keep a safe distance

However, it is not advisable to be completely cut off from these people and elements either. To be in the good books of a ruler is very beneficial. One learns a lot from religious teachers as they are treasure-troves of ancient wisdom. One cannot live without using fire on a day-to-day basis, be it for cooking or keeping warm. And for a man, life without a woman is fruitless. The best way to live with these people and elements is to not be too caught up in them. Be on your guard whenever you're dealing with any of the above.

6.24

**Without support wastes away a person
Even if he is brilliant and virtuous
For even a precious ruby
Shines bright when supported by a gold frame**

We all require support in life. It is only with the help of a support system does one becomes successful. A person without support can get lost in the fray.

Even the powerful require support

Without mentorship, a person can lose his direction. Even if a person is powerful, successful and virtuous, he needs counsel to avoid missteps.

A ruby shines brighter in the company of gold

The ruby is an expensive and precious stone. However, despite its beauty, it requires to be fixed in gold to be wearable, as part of a ring, necklace or even a crown. By itself, it can only be shut in a box, not flaunted. Effective mentorship is like the gold frame that holds the ruby. It lends the much-needed support and strength to the already brilliant jewel. So find a mentor who will support you like the gold frame that supports the ruby.

6.25

Many beings joined together
Can vanquish the enemy
As a bunch of straw fends off
The heavy downpour

Together we stand and divided we fall. When people are united, they have the strength to withstand any calamity that comes their way. Notice how a village comes together during a natural disaster. Never fight a battle alone, says Chanakya.

Join forces together

When one faces a powerful enemy, one should join forces with others who are threatened by the same menace. You may be weak on your own, but when you unite small groups, you can create a large and powerful army. A large, unified group with a common goal can vanquish a dangerous adversary.

A bunch of straw offering protection from rain

In ancient times, individual straws were bound together to make stacks that were used to pave the roofs of houses. These straw roofs protected people from heavy rains during the monsoons. Always remember that there is strength in numbers, so don't forget to ask for help when in need.

6.26

The one who betrays his own fraternity
And seeks refuge with the enemy
Brings about his own downfall
Like a kingdom without piety

Traitors never prosper. Those who desert their own to join the opposition thinking it will help them grow faster will be disappointed in the end, warns Chanakya.

The one who betrays his fraternity

We all belong to a fraternity. It could be our family, community or country. Fraternities are the very basis of our existence. Therefore, one should always be committed to one's group. One should never join the enemy camp, for any reason whatsoever.

A kingdom without piety

A deserter brings upon himself his downfall, says Chanakya. The one who betrays his people is never trusted again, not even in a new camp. Since he has already shown his true colours, his new friends will always be wary of his loyalty. Commit this to your memory: a person who is unable to get along with one group will not be accepted by others.

6.27

Save money for emergencies
But at the cost of money, protect your wife
However, protect your own life
At the cost of your wife and riches

What is money for? Money is of great importance during emergencies. However, to have money for emergencies, one must save it during good times. Even so, there are things dearer than money. Chanakya lists them in the order of their importance.

Save money

It is not important how much money you have earned. What counts is how much you have saved. Even if you earn a six-figure salary, and your savings account is empty, or God forbid, in the negative, you're still poor. Chanakya the economist introduced Indians to the 'saving culture' through his *neetis*. We all are indebted to him for this lesson.

Life over money

Money is, however, not everything. The money you have saved will be needed for emergencies. If your spouse or family is in trouble, save them at the cost of losing your savings. On the other hand, if your own life is in danger, Chanakya advises you to save yourself first at the cost of your spouse and money.

6.28

Even if without poison
A cobra may raise its hood
A raised hood is fearsome indeed
Even if devoid of venom

Nature has equipped every living being with essential tools for survival—it's the hood for the cobra and superior intelligence for humans. When in danger, it is only natural that your survival instincts overtake your general demeanour.

A cobra's hood

A cobra is feared when it raises its hood, even if it is a circus snake devoid of any venom. It's only natural to be afraid of a cobra poised to strike. It is our survival instinct at play. As the raised hood protects the cobra from any harm, man's intelligence protects him from impending danger.

Look fearsome, even if you don't mean it

When they say first impressions count, take it seriously. A cobra, even without its venom, looks threatening with its fanned hood. Similarly, use body language to create a persona that will help you stay in control in a competitive environment. Meek people don't survive. For people to take you seriously, you must first appear like you mean business.

6.29

Take alarm of the terrible
Till it hasn't drawn near
The terrible coming into view
Strike at it without fear

When you look into the eyes of the fear, the fear disappears. Fear is
a state of mind. If we can win over our mind, we can win over fear
too. Chanakya shows us the way to face fear.

Be aware

There are things that are terrible in this world. They also are
harmful to us. Be aware and alert about such terrible things. Do not
do anything about them till tyou are face to face with them.

Strike it when it comes near

When your fear materializes, strike at it. Don't hesitate. Your fears
hinder your progress; your fears keep you from living the life you
deserve. Know what troubles you. Search for the source of your
fears. Have the courage to achieve your goal, no matter how tough
the path. Remember that there is no gain without pain.

6.30

Giving as good as one gets
Measure for measure
One falls not from grace
By countering the aggressor

You should behave with others the way they behave with you; tit
for tat. This is the policy Chanakya followed all his life. And he is
advising you to do the same.

Give as good as you get

Observe how people treat you. Those who treat you with kindness should be treated with the same kindness. Those who torment you should be paid back in the same coin. Unkind people don't deserve your kindness. People should be held accountable for their actions.

Counter the aggressor

Never back down in the face of aggression. Stand up for yourself and make your voice heard. People tend to bully others, especially those who appear weak, to get their way. In a competitive environment this may happen frequently and one should be prepared to face people who use aggression to get what they want. Don't be a pushover. You views and opinions are important too. You have every right to say your piece without cowering.

6.31

**Deal cautiously with these six:
Fire, water, women, fools,
Serpents and members of the royal family
For they can bring about death quickly**

Keep away from dangerous elements. Being able to spot what is good for you and what is bad is the mark of maturity. Be wise in choosing what suits you best. Chanakya warns us about six such elements every man should be wary of.

Fire, water and women

You have to be careful with fire. It can burn you and destroy your possessions. So is the case with water. Be careful when stepping into unknown waters, you could drown. Women have to be treated with respect, or else you may end up behind bars.

Fools, serpents and members of the royal family

Fools don't pause to think. Interacting with fools is risky because they are impulsive and irrational. Poisonous serpents can attack unexpectedly. Anyone trying to outsmart a member of the royalty won't be tolerated. They are used to being obeyed and pampered. In addition, misinterpretations of behavior could prove deadly for those who are not from a privileged background.

6.32

**A king, a prostitute, Yama, fire,
A thief, a child and a beggar
Can't understand others' sufferings
The eighth among them is the tax collector**

Some people cannot empathize with others. They are too self-absorbed. Chanakya mentions eight such categories in this *neeti*.

A king, a prostitute, Yama, fire

A king is all powerful in his realm and can be insensitive to his subjects' needs. A prostitute thinks only of making money; each client is a business opportunity. The lord of death, Yama, ruthlessly takes people's lives without once caring about them or their loved ones. Fire will burn everything in its wake within seconds. It doesn't care about the suffering it causes.

A thief, a child, beggar and tax collector

A thief will steal from anyone. It doesn't matter to him if his victim is a virtuous man or not. A child will not stop throwing tantrums till his demands are fulfilled, no matter the circumstances. A beggar will approach anyone for alms; he doesn't care about societal hierarchy.

And the tax collector will not let anyone off without him paying his dues; he doesn't care about a bad harvest or drought.

6.33

**Kings pick men of good families
To serve them and to be around
For they don't forsake the kings
From beginning till end, through the thick of things**

Kings and men of power are always on the lookout for trustworthy aides. They recruit people who will be loyal in times of crisis. Always keep in mind that people of virtue will always be in demand, whether at royal courts or corporate houses.

People from good families

According to Chanakya, a good family background serves as a ticket to the most coveted jobs available. No, the master strategist is not referring to nepotism or favoritism here. His argument here is that candidates who have good credentials are sought after in the job market, especially by the ones in the upper echelons. In earlier days, a good pedigree was an assurance of a man's loyalty.

No deserters

Men of high moral values do not run away at the first sight of trouble. They stand their ground and serve their masters with the highest integrity. They are dependable; they stay till they are dismissed. All employers want employees who are reliable. They don't want job hoppers. So at work, build your credibility. Prove that your bosses can rely on you in challenging situations.

6.34

The hearts of mean men
Burn with the flame of others' fame
And they slander them, being unable to
Rise up to such heights themselves

In this *neeti*, Chanakya describes the mindset of a jealous person. Such people are available in plenty around us. Understand their thinking and be careful around them for they can be dangerous.

The flame of others' fame

When others are achieving something, those who are jealous cannot stand it. When others become famous, they burn inside. They cannot stand the success of others.

Slander the famous

One of the reasons people feel jealous of famous people or celebrities is that they are reminded of their own mediocre lives. Unable to develop to the level of winners, the jealous attempt to defame them.

6.35

He who neither causes fear when angered
Nor grant a favour when pleased
Can neither punish nor protect
What harm can he do?

He is considered powerful whom other people obey. The one who can control people based on his judgments is all-powerful. Those who don't have this control over others are powerless.

The one who causes no fear with his anger

Some personalities can put the fear of God into the object of their anger. Some people, no matter how angry they are, don't frighten others. When ineffective people are pleased, they can't confer any favours on others. They have no influence at all, and are not taken seriously.

Unable to punish or protect

Powerless leaders cannot punish or protect others, despite wishing to do so. Nobody listens to them, so they don't hold sway over anyone. What kind of life is that? It is better to be an achiever and influence others than be a nobody.

6.36

The wicked may develop
Good qualities in the presence of a good man
But the good person doesn't turn bad in the company of evil
The earth is scented by the flowers that fall upon it
But the smell of the earth doesn't touch the flowers

The goodness of a virtuous person does not disappear when he associates with the bad. Goodness always remains pure and also reduces the bad in others.

The company of the good

In the company of the good even a wicked person reforms. The good do not regress into bad behaviour in the presence of evil-doers. Wherever the good go, they remain good at all times and under all circumstances.

The fragrance of flowers

When fragrant flowers fall on the earth, they lend their fragrance to the ground, but do not acquire the smell of the earth. In the same way, wickedness doesn't colour the good and the virtuous. On the contrary, good men influence the malicious to change their course and walk the straight path. Always help the lost find their path.

6.37

**Sanctifying is the audience with a seer
For a seer is like a place of pilgrimage
Visiting a holy place is fruitful after a while
But meeting a seer is of instant advantage**

When one meets a sage, one gets purified instantly. It is like going to a place of pilgrimage. Even visiting a holy place is not comparable to meeting a living saint.

Audience with a seer

In Hinduism, spending time in the presence of a saint is known as having *darshan*. One feels purified and sanctified by his aura. Chanakya says that going to meet a saint is like going to a place of pilgrimage.

Holy place

Once you visit a temple, your prayers may be answered in time to come. But meeting a saint gives instant benefits, says Chanakya.

6.38

With the foot one may roll about a gem
One may wear mere glass as a crown
But in buying and selling, glass is glass
And gems remain as precious as ever

A gem is valuable no matter where it is placed. And glass is worthless even if it is embedded in a crown.

Gem and glass

A rare gem could be treated carelessly. And a king may wear a crown of glass for variety. The glittering glass may have a powerful visual impact, but it's effect is only temporary.

Buying and selling

A jeweller can differentiate between a precious gem and glass. Relatively speaking, the glass is worthless. On the other hand, precious gems are always valuable and not easily destructible. In the same way, Chanakya says the true value of a person is revealed at the appropriate time.

6.39

You may find pearls from the head of the elephant
If you walk into a lion's den
But in a jackal's lair
You will find only a calf's tail or pieces of donkey's fur

What you find depends on where you are looking. If you are searching for something particular, think beforehand where it could be found. Plan your search carefully. Without forethought, a search, however rigorous, will be fruitless.

A lion's den

The lion is the king of the jungle. Lions hunt prey larger than themselves because they are fearless and ferocious. So you may find a pearl or two from an elephant's head (it is an ancient belief that there are pearls inside a male elephant's head) in a lion's den. This shows the might of the predator.

A jackal's lair

Jackals are scavengers rather than hunters (even if they do hunt, they hunt only small prey). As a result, in a jackal's lair you will find only leftovers of a calf's tail or a donkey's skin. You won't find anything as majestic and precious as pearls from elephant heads there. Powerful people have trophies that befit them and ordinary people are happy with what they get.

6.40

**Not every mountain has rubies
Nor a pearl in the head of every elephant
Sages are not found everywhere
Nor sandalwood in every forest**

Certain valuable things are not easy to find. Chanakya here points out four things that are rare.

Rubies and pearls

In ancient lore, rubies are found on mountain tops. But not all mountains have rubies. So is the case with pearls found in the head of elephants; not every elephant has them. Be fastidious in your search. Know what you are looking for and anticipate where to find it.

Saints and sandalwood trees

Sages are not easy to come by. They dwell in holy places. Likewise, sandalwood trees can't be found in any and every forest. These are precious, sacred and rare. Finding them requires time and patience.

6.41

She who is chaste, clever,
Soft-spoken, truthful, pleasing to the husband
Is a true wife

Certain characteristics were valued in traditional Indian wives. A key quality was her devotion to her husband.

Chaste and clever

According to Chanakya, a good wife is chaste and deft. In other words, she is monogamous and is skillful in her household duties. She is intelligent and brisk in executing her chores.

Truthful, soft-spoken and pleasing to the husband

An honest wife doesn't hide anything from her husband, no matter how small the matter is. She takes delight in his companionship. She is soft-spoken and not arrogant. She takes care to behave in a way that pleases her husband. In traditional families, young girls were taught to aspire to these qualities as future wives.

6.42

A woman who fasts
Without the permission of her husband
Shortens his life
And she goes to hell

Here again Chanakya mentions practices followed by Indian women in ancient India. For a traditional wife, her husband was the center of her secular and spiritual life.

Women observing fasts and vows without permission

In ancient times, the husband was his wife's guardian. The wife had to usually take her husband's permission before she did anything important. Religious fasts were an integral part of an Indian woman's routine. A wife had to obtain her husband's permission before she undertook a fast or vow. This was done to strengthen the sacred bond of marriage. In this way, husband and wife were on the same page regarding household affairs and could work together towards any goal.

Reverse effect

According to Chanakya, if a wife undertakes a fast or vow without her husband's knowledge, it shortens his life. Mostly, married women prayed and fasted for the benefit of their husbands, especially for their longevity. Being a widow in ancient India was difficult, to say the least, and was considered inauspicious. So it was important for the wife to have a husband with a long life. If a husband dies young, his wife will have a difficult life as a widow, almost like hell on earth, says Chanakya.

6.43

**Honoured is a visiting king
Held in respect is a travelling Dvija;
A rambling yogi is paid homage
But a vagrant woman meets with outrage**

When you are independent, you are respected. Those who don't
settle down are disrespected.

Visiting king, travelling Brahmin, rambling yogi

A visiting king is honoured because he is a burden only for a short
time. He, therefore, enjoys good hospitality. A travelling *Dvija*
is treated with respect because he spreads wisdom and goodwill
wherever he goes. A wandering *yogi* is paid homage on his journey
for the same reason.

Vagrant woman

According to Chanakya, women should settle down once they reach
a marriageable age. A woman who doesn't settle down is a misfit and
is treated poorly by society. She is not respected and may encounter
many dangers because she is alone and unprotected. This is the
reason why marriage was considered an essential part of a woman's
life in ancient India.

6.44

One who eats without serving a traveler
Who has arrived at his door unexpectedly
From far away, tired and weary
Is a *Chandala*

Our culture is known for being welcoming and respectful to guests. *Athithi devo bhava;* we consider our guests to be gods.

The unexpected traveller

Sometimes people turn up at other people's houses without notice. A traveler who has come a long distance after a tiring journey deserves some warmth and care, even if he didn't send prior notice of his arrival.

Serve him

According to Chanakya, those who don't treat their surprise guests well are of base character. Give a tired traveler food and a place to rest. Make him comfortable. Anyone who eats first without serving such a traveller is despicable. He deserves only contempt.

6.45

Her husband is reverential for a wife
A guest is reverential for everyone in the house
Reverential is the fire for the *Dvija*
A *Dvija* is reverential for all classes of men

Who is respected and loved by people? It depends from person to person.

Husband and a guest

A wife respects her husband. The husband is expected to provide for his wife, children and the rest of the family. A guest in a household is respected by everyone in the family, and brings joy to it.

Fire and *Dvija*

A Brahmin reveres fire because he uses it for poojas and other rituals. Fire is essential for his livelihood. The Brahmin himself is respected across classes and communities for his wisdom.

6.46

**Speaking endearing words
Pleases all creatures
Therefore, O Honourable men!
We must use pleasing words
For there is no dearth of sweet words**

When one speaks politely, everyone is happy. Chanakya calls for more pleasant words in day-to-day communication.

Speaking endearing words

When one speaks endearing words, one's audience is pleased. No one likes to be criticized. Praise is welcome. One must know that positive words are pleasing in nature.

No dearth of sweet words

When you know that pleasant words deliver good results, why stop using them? Make it a habit to speak pleasantly and attract praise as well. The world today would be a better place if everyone followed this *neeti*, especially since our social media platforms are full of people spewing venom at one another.

6.47

Ignore the fool
For he is essentially a two-legged animal
Like an unseen thorn
He pierces the heart with his sharp words

No good comes out of keeping company with fools. They only utter nonsense and hurtful words. They don't deserve to be considered, according to Chanakya.

Ignore the fool

Intelligence makes human beings more evolved than animals. So if one speaks without thinking, one is nothing but an animal, a fool. According to Chanakya, a fool is not a human being but just a two-legged animal.

Sharp words that pierce the heart

Words hurt more than weapons. The wound inflicted by a weapon heals overtime, but harsh words once spoken remain with the listener for ever. Harsh words are like thorns that pierce an unsuspecting heart. A person who criticizes thoughtlessly causes far more grief than he realizes. Once spoken, harsh words can only be forgiven, not forgotten.

6.48

Win over the greedy with money
The haughty with showing courtesy
A fool by tickling his fancy
And a pundit with truth

Different ailments require different types of medicine. A good doctor knows that. Similarly, different types of people need to be handled differently.

The greedy and the haughty

The greedy are enticed only with money. No logic can convince a money-minded person. Give him money and his need is fulfilled. The arrogant have inflated egos. The best way to get a haughty person onto your side is by praising him. Show him courtesy and he will be cajoled easily.

A fool and a pundit

A fool lives in a fantasy world. He imagines himself to be far superior than he actually is. The best way to win over such an individual is to appreciate his fancy imaginations. A scholar is full of wisdom. The best way to win over a wise man is with honesty and humility.

6.49

The evil-minded and thorns
Can be met with two kinds of defences:
Either by breaking their faces with shoes
Or by keeping a safe distance

There are some people who cannot be won over at all. It is wise to give them what they deserve or keep away from them completely. No good can come from association with such people.

Evil-minded people and thorns

The wicked have been compared to thorns in this *neeti*. While a thorn may prick you while you are walking, the evil-minded can prick your happiness even when you are minding your own business. They can create unbelievable mental agony.

Two methods to overcome them

One should be able to defend oneself from evil-minded persons or thorns. This can be done in two ways, according to Chanakya: either by crushing them with footwear as you would kill an insect or by keeping a safe distance. These are the ways to protect yourself from harmful influences.

6.50

None in authority is free from aspiration
Not likely that the passionless is fond of ornamentation
Unlikely that a victim is well spoken
No way the deceitful is outspoken

When you are surrounded by certain people in particular circumstances, it is likely that you will be carried away.

People in power and passionless people

People in power are always aspirational. They are always looking for a higher position. A person who is not passionate is not interested in being fashionable. He doesn't seek admiration.

A victim and a deceitful person

An articulate person will not play the victim. Instead, he will stand up for what is right. He will fight for justice. On the other hand, a dishonest person is never straightforward. Since he has much to hide, he keeps his plans to himself.

6.51

Gentle manners should be learned from princes
The art of conversation from pundits
Falsehood should be learned from gamblers
And pretence from women

Chanakya's observations about people are very enlightening. He learns from everyone. Here he gives examples of four different kinds of people who can teach us about human nature.

Princes and pundits

Real princes are taught good etiquette, in preparation for their careers in court. From their gentle mannerisms, one can learn how to behave in public. Pundits or scholars are known for their well-articulated speech. They are able to hold the attention of their audience with their mesmerizing talks.

Gamblers and women

Good gamblers win through deception. Chanakya's views on women were archaic, so he says that women too get what they want through deceit. So learn from your surroundings; the world is your school.

6.52

**It's better to have no kingdom than the rule of tyranny
Better to have no friend than bad company
It's better to have no pupil than a stupid one
Having no wife is better than having a bitter one**

One should focus on quality in life. It is better not to have something rather than compromise on poor quality. Here Chanakya is pointing out how to make good choices in life.

Kingdom and friends

It is better to have no rule than the rule of tyranny. A tyrant is cruel and uses his power to harm others. It is better to have no king than have one like him. And it is better to be friendless than have rascals for company. They can cause trouble and spoil you as well.

Pupils and wife

Half-witted students waste a teacher's time and effort. There's no point in teaching those who don't partake in the process of learning. It is better to have no students than such poor ones. And it is better to be a bachelor than have a spouse who is not loving or loyal.

6.53

Renounce the religion falling short of compassion
Bid farewell to the guru lacking education
Leave alone the bitter wife
Let go of the kinfolk who doesn't show affection

Avoid, avoid, avoid. Those things that are harmful to you should be avoided at all cost. Otherwise they will steal your peace of mind and put you in troublesome situations.

Religion and guru

A religion that does not teach compassion is useless. If its teachings do not propagate peace and love, such a faith is harmful to society. A guru who is not learned is not fit to teach at all. If one is not educated, how will one person educate others? It is better to forsake such a teacher.

Wife and relatives

A bitter wife brings misery to her husband. She creates a negative environment at home. Your day will begin and end on a sour note. In addition those relatives who do not have affection for you should be kept at bay. What use are such relations? One can do without them.

6.54

He who lives in our hearts
Is near even though he may be far away
But he who is not on our mind
Is really far away even though he is nearby

In matters of love, distance is not an obstacle for people. For those who are not in love, they feel a distance, even if they are in close physical proximity.

Distance and heart

When someone is always in your thoughts, you will feel he is close to you even if he is miles away. Though the person could be in a different country or time zone, if he is in your heart, the physical distance feels immaterial. Loved ones always stay emotionally close, no matter how far away they are from each other physically.

Close but away

Two people who live in the same apartment but do not bond become strangers over time. Someone who is not close emotionally is not really close at all. The real closeness is in the intimacy of hearts.

6.55

On a full-grown tree
Birds of different feathers live together
At dawn, if they fly out in ten directions,
Why cry over it?

Family members live together in the same house for a long time. But at some point, some members go their own ways. This happens in every family, so don't feel pained about it. Move on with your life.

Birds on a tree

A large tree will house a number of different kinds of birds. The tree protects them from natural elements and predators. It gives them a place to rest. Though the birds are all different breeds, they forget their differences and find common refuge in the tree.

At dawn they fly away

These birds are together only for the night. In the morning, when they are refreshed, they fly out in different directions in search of food. Why should one bemoan this daily occurrence? At sunset they will be back to the tree again. In the same way, people grow out of their families and relationships and move on with their own individual lives. That's the natural order of things. There's no point grieving over this fact of life. When the need arises, dispersed families unite.

6.56

The cuckoo passes days
Remaining silent
In spring issues forth her voice
To everyone pleasant

It is better to be silent than make loud, unpleasant noises. Talk only when it is appropriate. Chanakya gives the example of the cuckoo bird to drive this point home.

Cuckoo remains silent

The cuckoo remains silent through most seasons. She is not easy to spot as she quietly goes about her day. Great men also work in the same manner. They don't articulate their opinions unless necessary. They go about their work without making a fuss.

Spring time

When spring comes, flowers bloom. There is beauty all around. During this period, the cuckoo starts singing in her beautiful voice. Everyone is pleasantly surprised. Her sweet song brings joy to one and all. Chanakya uses this analogy to teach you not to use your precious, God-given voice to say hurtful things. Instead, use your ability to speak up for the greater good.

6.57

**Living on fruits and roots of unploughed land,
Enjoying forest life constantly,
Performing shraddha every day,
Such a Brahmin is called a hermit**

A hermit lives a simple life. He eats food that is prepared without much effort and focuses on immersing himself in spiritual practices or *shraddha*.

Fruits and forest life

A hermit lives on fruits and roots that can be easily obtained. He farms for his subsistence. He enjoys his life in nature. He is content with very little.

Spiritual practices

Such a person is not considered lazy or a runaway. He performs his spiritual activities every day. He is completely focused on his spiritual quest. Such a person is a true Brahmin.

6.58

Busy with worldly affairs,
Tending cattle,
Engaged in commerce and agriculture,
Such a Brahmin is indeed a *Vaishya*

Here Chanakya discusses another kind of person. He may look like a Brahmin but his activities define him as a businessman rather than a spiritual seeker.

Busy with worldly affairs

This type of Brahmin is immersed in worldly affairs. He is engaged in agricultural and business activities.

A *Vaishya*

According to Chanakya, a Brahmin who engages in business activities becomes a *Vaishya*, a businessman. He may be a Brahmin by birth, but as soon as he steps into the world of business, he becomes a trader.

CHAPTER 7

SPIRIT OF THE TIMES

7.1

Women have appetites two-fold, Wisdom four-fold, courage six-fold, And passion eight-fold As compared to men

In the above *neeti*, Chanakya explains his perspective on women. Do bear in mind Chanakya lived at a time when women were considered inferior to men.

Appetite and wisdom

Chanakya says that women have twice the appetite of men. A woman not only feeds herself but also the child she will give birth to. According to Chanakya, a woman is also four times as intelligent as a man.

Courage and passion

Though women are perceived to be the weaker gender, they show their mettle in challenging times. Women stand up for a cause they believe in more boldly than men. They are eight times as passionate as men. When they set their heart on anything, they go after it with all they have got. In addition, they have a higher level of empathy than men. These qualities deserve respect.

7.2

Old lady, why are you gazing downwards?
Have you lost anything?
"O fool! Don't you understand?
The pearl of my youth has gone!"

With this verse Chanakya gives us an insight into what he thinks really matters to a woman. As she ages, she is always searching for something. What is it?

An old woman's quest

A stranger asks an old woman why she walks with her eyes to the ground. The man is curious to know whether she is searching for something.

The pearl of one's youth

No one wants to grow old, though aging is a natural process. The old woman replies to the man by saying that she has lost the pearl of her youth. Here youth is compared to a precious gem that one has lost and which one is trying frantically to regain. Just as we all do, the aging woman wants her youth back.

7.3

A whore will quit a poor man
The subjects will desert a defeated king
Birds will abandon a fruitless tree
And guests will leave the house after partaking in the meal

When you become useless and redundant, people will leave you. Chanakya uses this particular *neeti* to illustrate the transactional nature of certain relationships.

A prostitute and a king's subjects

A prostitute is not committed to one man. She maintains her clients for financial gain. If a customer suddenly cannot pay for her services, she will leave him. A powerless king cannot protect his subjects. His subjects have no use for him and will abandon him.

Birds and house guests

Birds frequent fruit-bearing trees. They will forsake a tree that once bore fruits but no longer does so. Similarly, a guest will leave his host's abode for his next destination after being served a sumptuous meal.

7.4

After receiving *dakshina*
The Brahmin leaves the worshipper
After receiving education, the student leaves his teacher
And animals leave the forest burnt down by fire

The idea in the previous *neeti* is continued here. Everyone has a time for being useful, an expiry date. When that time is over, others leave that person and continue on their journey.

The Brahmin after getting his *dakshina*

After he has completed his rituals, and is given *dakshina* (a token for his service), the Brahmin leaves the household of the worshippers.

Students and animals

Students go to a teacher for their education. Once their course is over, they leave the teacher. Only a few students keep in touch with their teachers post their student days. Likewise, animals desert the forest that is burnt to ashes. What use is such a forest if it doesn't provide them with food and shelter?

7.5

**Sins of the subjects are borne by the king
And those of the king are borne by the priest
The husband bears the sins of his wife
And the pupil's sins are borne by the teacher**

If one commits a sin, it is someone else that bears the responsibility for it. Chanakya gives three such examples here.

The king and the priest

It's the king's obligation to bear the sins of his subjects. As their ruler, he's responsible for their actions, good or bad. If some citizens commit immoral acts, their results affect their king and kingdom. In turn, it is the king's priest who has carries the burden of the ruler's sins because he is the king's advisor on most matters.

Students and husbands

If some students live degenerate lives, their teacher will be held responsible for their behaviour. It's the teacher's job to teach his students the difference between good and bad. Likewise, when a wife commits a sin, it is her husband who has to suffer. Once a wife pledges herself to her husband in marriage, her mistakes are her husband's responsibility. This is because he has in turn pledged to take care of her.

7.6

The lamp eats darkness
And produces soot
Likewise, the food you usually eat
Determines the quality of your offspring

The saying "you are what you eat" is quite popular. But here, Chanakya goes one step further and says, "Your children are what you eat." Let's take a look at the example given.

Lamp and soot

When a lamp is lit, it drives darkness away. When the lamp runs out of oil, and the wick burns out, only soot remains.

Food and offspring

We get nutrients from what we eat. In Ayurveda, our diet is categorized into three types: *rajasic*, *tamasic* and *sattvic*. *Rajasic* food is overly spicy and causes restlessness, stress and anger. *Tamasic* food causes lethargy. *Sattvic* food is simple, healthy and balanced. What you eat is absorbed by your body and becomes part of your constitution. Your genes, which are products of what you eat, are passed to your children and affect the strength of their constitution.

7.7

Generosity, soft speech,
Equanimity and rectitude
Are not gained by recitation
But through hard work and experience

Certain qualities cannot be acquired by merely proclaiming you have them. For example, if a person keeps repeating, "I am wise," it does not make him wise. One develops good qualities through hard work and experience, over a period of time.

Generosity, soft speech, equanimity and rectitude

These are qualities that are highly cherished and people with these virtues tend to do well in life in the long run. However, one is not born with good qualities; they are acquired along the way. Moreover, they're not easy to attain.

Mere recitation is pointless

Good qualities are developed only through hard work and experience. No one becomes good or generous by merely wishing so. One gains wisdom through a wide range of experiences and exposure. If you only dream of being soft-spoken but don't practice such a manner of speaking when you interact with people, how is that of any consequence?

7.8

Whose family is without blemish?
Who is free from sickness and grief?
Who hasn't come across calamity?
Who is happy forever?

Nothing is perfect or permanent in life. Each one of us goes through our own ups and downs. Chanakya explains to the reader that no one is flawless or lives an ideal life.

Family, sickness and grief

In this world there is no family without defects. There is nothing called a perfect or ideal family. Individuals in every family quarrel and later make-up with each other. Discord is normal and a part of human behaviour. Who has not suffered from diseases or grief in life? Ailments are also a part of life, especially when one grows old. One has lived a full life only when one has balanced the good with the bad.

Calamity and happiness

Is there a single person in this world who has not faced calamities in life? Everybody faces the death of near and dear ones. Sometimes, even the loss of wealth and property. Life is not always a song-and-dance affair. Happiness and sorrow come and go. If you observe closely, you will notice that they follow each other. Understanding the patterns of life will give you the perspective required to lead an emotionally stable life.

7.9

Oil on water; a secret confided in the treacherous;
Donation to the deserving, even in small measures;
And knowledge in a wise person
Expand by themselves because of inherent nature

Some things can't be contained; they expand naturally. In this
neeti, Chanakya gives a few examples to show us the innate nature
of expansion. It could be good or bad, but if it is meant to spread,
it will.

Oil, secrets and donation

When you pour oil on water, the oil spreads on the surface of the
water. In the same way, a secret shared with a gossip monger spreads
like wildfire. Never share your secrets with unreliable people.
Likewise, donations given in even small quantities to those in need
result in the spreading of the donor's goodwill.

A wise person's knowledge

Knowledge is ever-expanding, and so much so in the case of a
learned person. Such a person spreads his knowledge further and
thus creates more awareness wherever he goes. Knowledge is the
light that dispels the darkness of ignorance and a well-educated
person is the torch-bearer.

7.10

**A fool envies the pundit
The impoverished covets the wealthy
The unfortunate envies the fortunate
And a flirt envies the chaste**

Envy is a part of human nature. You develop jealousy when you compare yourself with others who you feel are better than you.

Fools and the impoverished

Ignorant fools envy those who are learned. An uneducated person may feel inferior to a scholar and thus envy his standing in society. The poor aspire to be rich; they feel envious of the wealthy. A poor man may feel the rich have comfortable and ideal lives cushioned by their wealth. One always envies what one doesn't have and forgets about what one does have.

The unfortunate and the flirt

Those who feel unfortunate are jealous of those they think are lucky. In their eyes, the fortunate get wealth and services effortlessly. A flirt is envious of those who remain committed to their partners, and have a steady and long-lasting relationship. The flirt flits from one lover to another, yet he remains dissatisfied with his relationships. True love eludes him.

7.11

**Without a child, a family is void
Without kinfolk, quarters are void
The mind of a fool is void
And the poor is void of everything**

Life is incomplete without some key things, says Chanakya. Without them, what use is such a life?

Children and relatives

Children complete a family and bring joy to their parents. They fill a house with laughter and commotion and turn it into a home. Also, what is a home without relatives to live with? You may have a large house, but if there's nobody to occupy it, what use is it?

Fools and poor people

There is nothing inside the mind of a fool. It is totally empty. What use is he? An impoverished person's life is devoid of material pleasures. He can't buy anything for himself or his loved ones and this leaves him feeling unhappy always.

7.12

**Though born of the same womb
And under the same constellation
Like the thorns of a jujube shrub
Two persons are never the same in their disposition**

Two people are never alike, even if they are identical twins. Each person in this world has a unique personality and that is what makes the world so diverse.

Born from the same womb

Identical twins have the same mother and are born under the same constellation, yet they have different identities and personalities.

Like the thorns on a jujube shrub

Any two people will always have different qualities and character. They can be compared to the thorns of the jujube shrub. This plant has many thorns. Thorns grow from the same stem and have common roots, yet each thorn is different from the other.

7.13

**Ripening of age notwithstanding
Bitterness in the wicked does endure
As the fruit of *indravaruni*,
Despite ripening remains sour**

Some people remain as they are forever. Their inherent nature does not change with age. One is expected to mature with age. Alas, all men do not evolve with time.

Maturity

With age comes maturity and wisdom (or so they say). Old age is a marker of experience. As one sees more of life, one naturally becomes kinder towards others. Good qualities emerge in an ordinary person with time.

The wicked ones

Unfortunately, wicked people do not change with age or experience. Their bitterness is a part of their unchanging nature. Chanakya compares such people to the *indravaruni* fruit which is sour even after it ripens.

7.14

Of all medicines, *amrit* is the best
Of all comforts, food is excellent
Of all sense organs, eyes are the most important
Of all parts of the body, head is the topmost

Among the masses, those with class stand out. One can easily differentiate the extraordinary from the ordinary. What makes them special?

Medicines and comforts

In Hindu mythology, *amrit* is considered the best medicine as it can make man immortal. In such a condition, what more is there to cure?

One can have many comforts, but nothing beats enjoying a good meal when hungry. Food which is well prepared and tasty is the supreme luxury.

Eyes and head

Among our sensory organs, the eyes are the most important. Navigating this complex world for a blind man is excruciatingly difficult. Our body has many parts. Yet the head with our brains is on top of the list and is literally on top of our body. Our brain makes all the decisions for the rest of our organs. Through this analogy about the bests in various categories, Chanakya inspires us to be the best in whatever we do.

7.15

**Flour is ten times more nutritious than corn
But milk is ten times better than flour
Black gram is ten times better than milk
And still ghee is ten times better**

Health is wealth. Only if you eat healthy will you live long, be productive and contribute to the betterment of the world. So watch what you eat. Choose your food after understanding the nutritional value of each ingredient. Chanakya gives an example here.

Flour, corn and milk

Corn is the food of the poor. In many developing countries, people live on corn. However, corn lacks some key nutritional elements. Flour, which is a staple in Indian kitchens, is 10 times more nutritious than corn. However, milk is even more nutritious than flour.

Black gram and ghee

The black gram is a type of bean grown in the Indian subcontinent. It is packed with vitamins and proteins, so much so that it is 10 times more nutritious than milk. But according to Chanakya, our common ghee is the most nutritious of all.

7.16

Diseases spread from raw vegetables
The body grows with milk
Virility grows with ghee
Strength grows with meat

A strong body houses a healthy mind. Taking care of your body is
of utmost importance. Know what to eat and what to avoid. Treat
your body like a temple.

Vegetables and milk

Vegetables are good for the body. However, but according to
Chanakya, they have to be cooked, not eaten raw. Cleaning and
cooking vegetables kill harmful microorganisms that may live in
them. Milk is nutrient-rich and essential for the growth of one's
bones and teeth. Babies are given milk to foster their rapid growth
and maintain a healthy constitution.

Virility and strength

Virility refers to manliness. In order to be a strong human being,
Chanakya suggests that we include ghee in our diet. Meat ensures
a robust body because it is rich in vitamins, minerals, antioxidants
and other nutrients.

7.17

The weak become hermits
The poor remain celibate
A sufferer takes to piety
The old lady remains loyal

At times we accept certain circumstances not because we like them, but because we cannot avoid them. Chanakya provides examples of people who are forced to live in a particular way.

The weak and the poor

The weak, owing to their feeble health, become hermits, says Chanakya. They attempt to survive by begging. Their weak constitution makes it difficult for them to perform physical labour— hence they beg. The poverty-stricken remain celibate; who will marry a poor man? In ancient India, only the rich could afford marriage.

The sufferer and the old lady

A suffering person is forced to be humble. Since he's dependent on the goodwill of others, what else can he do? An old lady remains devoted to her husband because few will fancy her at her age. In these examples, it is not the choice of the people involved but their circumstances that dictate what kind of life they lead.

7.18

Trivial is heaven for the one who has known the self
Trivial is life for the brave-hearted
Trivial are women for the one with subdued senses
And trivial is the world for the disinterested

Inconsequential are all successes of the world to one who has achieved everything. For one who has satisfied his hunger, no food can tempt him. Once your desires are fulfilled, you are at peace with yourself and the world.

Heaven and life

The joys of heaven are insignificant for a person who has gained self-knowledge.

The self-realised soul is not attracted to external and material pleasures for he has found joy within himself. For a brave man, death is of little consequence. He is willing to give his life for his goals.

Women and the world

When one's senses are in control, sensuality loses its lustre. For a man whose senses are subdued, women do not hold sway. For those who are disinterested in material life, the world and its pleasures are unimportant. Such a person is in the world but not of it.

7.19

**If the king is virtuous, then the subjects are also virtuous
If the king is sinful, then the subjects also become sinful
If he's mediocre, then the subjects are also mediocre
The subjects follow the king
As the king, so are his subjects**

As the king so the people of his kingdom; as the leader so his followers. The quality of the followers depends on the quality of the leader they have.

Virtuous, sinful or mediocre

When the king is righteous, his subjects automatically become upright. When the king is corrupt, his people will embrace corruption as well. An unethically run kingdom will plunge into chaos. A mediocre leader has no chance of building a team of brilliant advisors.

As the king so his people

Great kings in our past set high standards for governance and codes of ethics for their subjects.

Today, if we all set high standards of leadership for ourselves, then our cumulative efforts will ensure we live in a great society.

7.20

Constant travel tires a man
Horses get tired being tied up always
A woman ages quickly when not with her husband
Clothes become old when left in the sun for too long

Too much of anything is not good. One gets worn out with prolonged activities. Life is to be enjoyed in moderation.

Man and horses

Constant travel is exhausting. It's is natural to feel sluggish after travelling extensively. Our bodies are not built for enduring long periods of travel. On the other hand, if a horse is tethered for long, it gets tired. Horses are active animals and were a major means of transport in the past. Every animal, including humans, is built differently. One has to understand one's limits and act accordingly.

Women and clothes

A woman who lives long periods of time away from her husband ages quickly. She is unhappy in her separation and suffers without the refreshing love of her husband. Washed clothes are put out in the sun to dry. But if you leave them in the sun for too long, their colour will fade and they will resemble old rags. The lesson here is moderation in everything is the key to living a successful life.

7.21

Tundi weakens the mind
Vacha strengthens it instantly
A woman weakens the vigour of a man
But is restored swiftly with milk

In this verse, Chanakya shows that every problem has an antidote;
you only have to look for it.

Tundi and *vacha*

Chanakya says that *tundi* (a type of gourd) weakens the mind, but
vacha (calamus) boosts the mind. Both are plant-based products.
However, their properties are so different from each other. One
reverses the effect of the other.

Women and milk

Chanakya says spending time with women weakens a man's vigour.
However, this can be easily restored with milk. Milk is a protein-
packed food and a good source of calcium and other minerals. It
restores energy and helps one stay healthy and fit.

7.22

The bee who is used to lying on the soft petals of the
lotus flower
And drinking sweet nectar in abundance
Is now drinking from the ordinary *kutaja* flower
Being in a foreign land where there are no lotuses
He is considering the *kutaja* grove grand

You have to make do with what you get. When circumstances
change, the best strategy is to adapt rather than complain. Chanakya
uses the example of a honey bee here to drive home his point.

Bee and the lotus flower

The lotus is considered one of the most beautiful flowers in the
world. In Hinduism, it is also considered sacred. A bee, who is used
to drinking nectar from lotuses and buzzing around their soft petals,
is indeed living a life of luxury.

In a foreign land

If this bee is displaced and is forced to live in an environment
without lotuses, he has to satisfy himself with whatever flowers exist
in that region, even if they are *kutaja* flowers. *Kutaja* is a common
flower variety. But when in need, the *kutaja* is also a friend indeed.
One has to adapt to one's circumstances. Those who resist change
don't survive. So like the bee in this example, be flexible. Don't
cling to your past; move on with your life.

7.23

Ash cleans brass
Acid cleans copper
Periods clean a woman
And flowing water cleans a river

Impurities can be cleansed. If one is determined to find a way to be good, one will find it for sure. Like an antidote to a poison, find what cleanses you.

Ash and acid

Brass is cleaned with ash, while copper can be cleaned with acid. Even though both brass and copper are metals, they require different cleaning agents. The same goes for people. As no two men are alike, their vices will also drastically differ. One has to choose the appropriate method for ridding oneself of a particular set of bad habits.

Periods and flowing water

Women go through a natural cleaning process during their menstrual cycles every month. Similarly, the flowing water in a river keeps the river clean. If water remains stagnant, the river will be overrun with algae and become unusable. Everybody needs to undergo a cleaning process periodically, be it spiritual, physical or lifestyle-related. Know what vices need to be uprooted from within you and choose a cleansing process that suits you.

CHAPTER 8

—

EVERYTHING
BENEFICIAL

8.1

One good son
Educated and upright
Delights the whole family
As the moon lights up the night

It is better to have one child who is useful than many insolent children. Chanakya gives us a compelling parenting tip in this *neeti*: bring up well-behaved and educated children.

One good son

Historically, families preferred sons to daughters, because the sons would inherit the family wealth and carry the family name forward. Daughters were married off at a young age, so they didn't belong to their biological family. Our ancestors, therefore, longed for many sons. But here Chanakya says it is not the number of the sons that matters but their quality. So it is better to have one son who is educated and morally upright, rather than many uneducated and immoral children.

The moon at night

Having well brought up children is a matter of pride for the clan. As the moon lights up the night, such offspring will delight the entire household. So even if the child is from a poor or humble background, he brings hope for the family if he is cultured and well-educated.

8.2

Why to beget many sons
Who cause grief and agony?
Better is one son as the pillar
On whom rests the whole family

The idea discussed in the previous *neeti* is discussed further here. Why do you need to have many sons when you can have one good son who becomes the source of happiness for all?

Many sons

It is up to the parents to decide how many children they want to have. So why have many sons or children, who will later cause grief and agony? It is challenging to bring up children well and it can be a stressful and painful experience as well.

One son as the pillar of the family

Today, it is important to have a son or a daughter who becomes the pillar of the family based on the strength of his or her character. Parents, when they become old, depend on their children for support. Just like a strong pillar, good offspring shoulder the burdens of the family and protect and provide for it.

8.3

Better is one virtuous son
Than a hundred duds
For one moon dispels the darkness
But not the stars in thousands

It is better to have one virtuous son instead of a hundred without merit. And to drive home his point, Chanakya compares one moon with a thousand stars.

One virtuous son

Children who are virtuous and ethically upright are key to a stable family. They are well-mannered and well-behaved. It is better to have one righteous son rather than a hundred wastrels, who are disappointments to their parents, says Chanakya.

The moon and the stars

It is better to have one moon that dispels the darkness of the night than a thousand stars that do not light up the sky. Only the moon is capable of showering a significant amount of light. A good son is like the full moon; he brings light and happiness to the entire family.

8.4

**Of the worldly sufferings
These three lessen the strain:
Worthy children, affectionate wife,
And the company of good people**

The world is full of suffering, and it feels like being in the middle of the ocean with no shore in sight. But luckily there are places where one can find some respite.

Worldly sufferings

No one escapes the sorrows of life. Everybody goes through some trial or the other; nobody has an entirely smooth journey. Always remember that pain is a part of life. So what can one do to alleviate worldly suffering?

Children, wife and good company

Chanakya points out three elements that can reduce the strains of
the world and suffering. What are they? First comes one's children.
For a parent, good-mannered and caring children are like a salve on
a hurting wound. The second is an affectionate wife. A spouse who
listens to all your grievances with patience is a great asset. Lastly,
good friendships are vital to get through one's miseries. Genuine
friends help each other out during tough times. So make sure you
have a few friends you can count on.

8.5

Nothing equals giving food and water in charity
No day is more auspicious than *dvadasi*
No incantation out does the Gayatri mantra
No deity is superior to one's own mother

There are some things that are auspicious and superior among the
rest in their respective categories. They can't be ignored.

Charity and *dvadasi*

In Indian culture, charity is given a lot of importance. Nothing can
equal giving food and water to the needy. Feeding the hungry and
quenching the thirst of the parched should be high in priority for
those looking to do some good in life. Also, among the days, *dvadasi*
(the 12th day of the lunar calendar) is considered very auspicious.

Gayatri mantra and mother

Among the various chants that we have in the Vedic tradition,
the Gayatri mantra is the most important and auspicious, says
Chanakya. And no deity or god is more superior to one's own

mother. Therefore, respect your mother and take care of her; treat her like you would treat a deity and not as an ordinary human being.

8.6

**Blessings though good deeds, wealth, food grains,
One's guru's words and medicine
Stock them up as much as possible
Without them, life becomes impossible!**

When travelling to far-off lands, it is prudent to carry a kit stacked with essentials. Who knows when it'll come handy. Chanakya talks about such a survival kit for life here. Let's look at its contents.

Blessings, wealth, food grains, guru's words and medicine

Good deeds result in blessings. These blessings are essential to overcome the challenges in life successfully. Money and food are also critical for one's survival, so always save for a rainy day. Never have an empty kitchen. Stock it up well. No one can predict what tomorrow will be like. Hunger can strike even the wealthy during a calamity. Just like blessings, one's spiritual teacher's words are a source of solace and inspiration. Apart from these four things, always keep a first-aid kit ready. During an emergency, all these preparation will save you life.

Stock up the essentials

Ensure that you heed the above mentioned advice. No one can predict the future, so you don't know what's in store for you. Having your basic needs covered is half the battle won.

8.7

**Friendship amongst equals flourishes
Service under the royals is respectable
Business is good among occupations
And a beautiful woman is safe at home**

One must know one's place in a gathering. A crow will be out of place among the swans. Trying to fit in with the wrong kind will not help you in any way. On the contrary, it may harm your future.

Friendship and service

Friendship among equals is the only kind that flourishes. Seeking friends among those who are of higher social status than you or those who are from the lower strata of society than you will not work simply because you will be a misfit in both sets. So people who belong to the same social class get along well together. On the other hand, if you have to work under someone, who better than someone far higher in status than you, such as royalty? Serving the king is indeed a prestigious affair.

Business and beauty

During Chanakya's time, the trader community was prosperous than the labour community. Workers were paid poorly and were made to toil. So owning a business was considered a better career option than hard labour.

According to Chanakya, a beautiful woman is safer at home than outside because her beauty may attract miscreants on the streets. She may come in harm's way because of her good looks. Of course, sitting at home to keep safe from harm is not applicable to today's women, so be on your guard when on the move, belles!

8.8

Wealth preserves piety
Learning is preserved by application
Tenderness preserves the king
And a home is preserved by a well-behaved woman

What is the best way to preserve the things you love or have earned with much hard work? Chanakya provides some insight into the matter.

Piety and learning

Devotion and righteousness are preserved by wealth. If one's basic needs are not met, one won't be interested in spirituality or charity. For a person to walk the right path, having money helps. Book-based learning is of no use if it's not applied in real life. Without application, knowledge is worthless; it is mere theory.

King and home

What keeps the king and his power intact? It is his tenderness and humility. If the powerful are humble, others respect them and adore them. Our history is full of brutally defeated tyrants and beloved rulers who were good to their subjects. Like a good ruler preserves his kingdom, a home is preserved by a good homemaker. It's women who turn a house into a home, a piece of heaven on earth.

8.9

Knowledge is a friend when away from home
Wife is a friend at home
Medicine is a friend when sick
Piety remains a friend at the time of death

Who are your real friends? Those who are helpful in the time of need. Having an understanding of who your real friends are will help you weed out those who are close to you only for their benefit.

Knowledge and wife

Someone who is well-educated is never alone on the road of life. His knowledge accompanies him everywhere. So you may not know anyone in a foreign country, and yet the knowledge you have acquired will keep you safe. While at home, your wife is your best friend. In the company of a good wife, you will find happiness and comfort.

Medicine and piety

Medicines that provide you relief are your real friends during a bout of sickness. And at last, on the death bed, only true devotion and the merits you have acquired through your admirable deeds will be by your side.

8.10

The power of the king is in his mighty arms
The power of the Brahmin is in his spiritual knowledge
And the power of a woman is in her beauty, youth and
sweet temperament

What is power? The answer: it depends. Power is very contextual. It varies from one person to another. Three examples are given here.

The king and the Brahmin

The power of the ruler is in the size of his army and the quality and quantity of the arms he possesses. His vigour, enthusiasm and valour keeps him in power. Likewise, spiritual knowledge is the power of a Brahmin. He knows all there is to know about prayers and rituals to please the gods. A well-prepared king and a well-educated Brahmin are both difficult to defeat.

A woman's power

The power of a woman is in three things according to Chanakya: her beauty, youthfulness and sweet temperament. Though the standard of beauty and the stigma of ageing are not the same today as it was during Chanakya's time, the definition of a good-natured person hasn't changed. Whether a man or woman, a sweet-tempered person is loved by all.

8.11

**Like a whole forest becomes fragrant
By a single tree with sweet flowers blossoming
A family becomes famous with the birth
Of a virtuous son**

It is not quantity but quality that matters most. Just a few grains of salt can turn a bland dish tasty. So it is with people; the good ones always count.

A tree with sweet blossoms

Just one tree's aromatic flowers can turn the whole forest fragrant. Good things aren't required in truckloads to prove their worth; even small quantities are effective.

One good son

Similarly, one good son's success brings glory to his entire family. One virtuous child can make a big difference to his entire clan and community. Other family members and friends can also take pride in being associated with such a noble individual.

8.12

**He whose sons are obedient
Has a pleasing wife
And is content with wealth
Is able to experience heaven on earth**

One can experience heaven on earth. There's no need to wait till one dies! One can find heavenly happiness here and now, says Chanakya, if one has the following:

Sons and wife

Obedient children are godsends; they make life a treat for their parents. On the other hand, nasty, ill-behaved children are a parent's nightmare. So count yourself blessed if your child is disciplined and respectful towards others. So too, if you have a pleasing wife to share your joys and sorrows with.

Wealth

If you are content with the money you earn and your bank balance, you are a rare breed. The entire world is scurrying to make more money. If you can be satisfied with what you have, nothing can upset you. Contentment is real happiness; greed can make people restless. If you already have all the above, then you have found heaven on earth; there is nothing more to experience in your afterlife.

8.13

**If one has a lovely wife and wealth in plenty,
Gentle and meritorious offspring,
Grandchild in the family,
Is there anything more in heaven?**

India's foundation is its family-oriented culture. For us, family is everything. We experience heavenly pleasure when our family members are noble and successful.

Wife and wealth

If your wife is devoted to you, brings you joy and is with you through thick and thin, then you are a lucky man. If you are also wealthy and you are content with your wealth, that's a bonus. Such a person does not need to care about what heaven has to offer.

Children and grandchildren

In addition, if you have dutiful and virtuous children and are blessed with grandchildren, what more do you want? You are already in paradise. You are living a fairytale life most people can only dream of.

8.14

A happy home, intelligent children,
A charming and soft-spoken wife,
Wish-fulfilling wealth, conjugal bliss,
Servants who obey the orders,
Hospitality to guests, worship of Shiva daily,
Delicious food and drinks for the family,
Always enjoying the company of good people,
Blessed is indeed the state of this householder

A blessed householder has nothing to complain about. From all perspectives, he is living a fulfilled life. Chanakya gives a list of things that makes such a person happy indeed.

A happy home, children, wife, wealth, love

A joyful family, intelligent and studious children, a charming and soft-spoken wife, enough wealth, marital bliss—all these are highly desirable for a householder.

Guests, worship, food, the company of good people

A house where guests are treated hospitably and Lord Shiva is worshipped daily becomes a temple itself. And above all, if the householder enjoys the company of noble people, he is even further fulfilled.

CHAPTER 9

———

SINISTER ELEMENTS

**Practicing what is in the scriptures wrongly is poison
Food is poison when undigested
A social gathering is poison to a pauper
A young wife is poison to an old man**

Poison needn't come in a bottle with statutory warnings. Certain circumstances can turn poisonous, threatening your wellbeing. Chanakya gives some such examples here.

Scriptures and food

How can these two things be poisonous, you ask. When scriptures are wrongly recited, they become toxic. An incorrect interpretation of holy texts can be misleading. Therefore, study the scriptures in the right context and do not mislead others with inaccurate interpretations. Likewise, food provides nutrition, only if it is prepared and digested well. Undigested food can be harmful for the body.

Pauper and old man

When one is poor, social gatherings don't bring joy. One naturally compares oneself with others and feels inferior to the ones who are more successful. Whatever upsets your peace of mind is toxic. In another example, the relationship between an old man and a young wife could become heavily strained because of the age difference between the two. His youth is gone. Without youthful energy, he may not be able to entertain and engage his young wife as would a youngster of her age. The old husband will lose his confidence and self-respect in trying to impress his young bride. Therefore, for him, the company of a young girl is disastrous.

9.2

The poison of a snake is lodged in its fangs
The poison of a fly is in its head
The scorpion has poison in its tail
The poison in the wicked is all over

Many life forms are poisonous. But one thing that separates them from a vile person is that one knows exactly where such creatures store their venom.

Snake and fly

The poison of a snake is in its fangs. And snake catchers know how to remove poison from its fangs without hurting the reptile. Likewise, a fly carries its poison in its head.

Scorpion and wicked people

In the case of a scorpion, the poison is in its tail. The scorpion stings with its tail to paralyze its prey with poison. But in the case of the wicked person, there is no specific place where he stores his venom. It's spread throughout his personality.

9.3

Foolishness is annoying
The youth too are indeed annoying
But the most annoying thing is
Living in another's house

It is natural to feel annoyed. Everyday life presents myriad opportunities for us to get irritated. But some are more annoying than the others. Let's see how.

Foolishness and youth

Interacting with a fool is tiresome. It is frustrating when someone doesn't understand, or worse, misunderstands your ideas or actions. An uneducated person is unable to grasp the nuances of communication. Such interactions get annoying. The same is the case with some young people. They don't conform to rules; they do as they please. They also believe that youth is forever and act foolishly and rashly. It is, therefore, annoying to interact with such arrogant youngsters.

To live in another's house

One is just a guest anywhere but one's own home. And when one overstays one's welcome, naturally one's host isn't going to be pleased. Looking after a guest is a stressful affair; taking good care of the guest and his needs day after day requires patience and effort. Very few people can devote their time to such an activity for long. This displeasure will reflect in the host's relationship with the guest, making the stay unpleasant for both parties. So it's best to keep one's visit short if one wants to maintain the relationship, no matter how strong a bond one shares with one's host.

9.4

**Where one finds no respect,
No means of livelihood, no kinsmen,
And no means of education
That place is not fit for habitation**

For a place to be hospitable, it must have certain characteristics. These elements are non-negotiable, says Chanakya. Otherwise, the residents will suffer in the long term.

Respect, livelihood, kinsmen and education

Imagine living in a place where no one respects you. Imagine a place where there aren't any opportunities to earn your own livelihood. Imagine a place where you do not have relatives or friends. Now imagine that this place doesn't have any opportunities for education. Do you think such a place is worth living in?

No place for habitation

Before selecting a place to live, people usually assess its pros and cons. It is a good practice. On that list, respect comes first. Living in a humiliating or disrespectful atmosphere is akin to death. If you are planning to settle down in a particular area, it is important that you have easy access to all important amenities. There must be adequate education and job opportunities. You must live near friends so you can turn to them when you are in need. Schools and colleges must be close to your neighbourhood. If your residence at present doesn't offer you these facilities, it's time to move out.

9.5

**Do not stay even for a day in a place
That doesn't have these five:
A king, a Brahmin, a rich man,
A river and a doctor**

The worth of a place can be assessed by knowing who lives there and what resources it has. Chanakya gives a list of five things that makes any place livable or even worth considering as your home.

A rich person, a Brahmin and a king

A financially poor locality has no scope for prosperity. A place without a Brahmin or a spiritual teacher, is a place devoid of morals.

Righteous people can't survive there. Here, "king" refers to someone of authority and power. Without law and order, a place descends into chaos sooner or later.

A river and a doctor

Water is the very source of life. And a hospitable place requires a perennial source of water to sustain its inhabitants. The river is such a source. And one needs a doctor and a hospital in one's vicinity. No point in travelling long distances for medical help. So if these five characteristics don't exist in a particular place, avoid it.

9.6

A house where a Brahmin's feet are not washed
Where scriptures are not read
Where holy rites of *svaha* or *svadha* are not performed
Such a house is like a cremation ground

A house is not just a structure made of brick and mortar. It is not just about fancy furniture and beautiful interiors. A house is much more than that. According to Chanakya, the best house has a spiritual angle to it.

Brahmin and the recitation of scriptures

It is considered auspicious to have a Brahmin visit one's house. Such guests are welcomed in traditional style, by the host washing the feet of the esteemed guest. Also, reciting scriptures in the house either at dawn or dusk is beneficial for the entire family. This recitation is said to dispel negative energy and usher in good fortune.

Svaha and svadha

Svaha here refers to holy rituals practiced to appease God and *svadha* refers to the rites performed in memory of dead ancestors. Both the blessings of God and one's ancestors are given importance in Indian culture. Chanakya compares a house where such spiritual activities are not practiced to a cremation ground—a highly polluted environment in Hinduism.

9.7

Tell me, O *Vipra*, who in this town is the greatest?
"A palm grove!"
Who is the best donor?
"A washerman who returns the clothes in the evening!"
Who is the cleverest?
"The one robs the wealth or the wife of another!"
How do you survive in a place like this?
"Like a worm in poisoned bread!"

In the above conversation between two people, one is a learned man, and the other, perhaps a traveller. The traveller quizzes the wise man about a city and its inhabitants.

Palm grove and washerman

The traveller asks the wise man: who is great in the city? The palm grove, answers the wise man. A palm grove gives shade and a place to rest for a tired traveller for free. In that sense, a group of palm trees is the greatest comfort for the traveller.

Next the traveller asks who the most charitable person in the city is. To this, the wise man says, a washerman. He washes his customer's dirty clothes and returns them by evening. For a traveller who doesn't want to be held up in one place, isn't that one of the most useful services he could utilize?

Thieves and worms

Who is the cleverest among men, asks the traveller. According to the wise man, anyone who steals the other person's wife or wealth is clever. A person's family and his fortunes make him worthy in the eyes of society, so he will protect them with all his might. So someone who can rob a man off his dearest possessions has to be the sharpest. The traveller again asks about the kind of life in a city where all these things happen. The wise man compares the city to poisoned bread and himself to a worm that survives on such bread. Here the point is that only the toughest survive in a challenging environment.

9.8

**What use is the cow
That neither gives milk nor conceives?
What use is a son
Who is neither learned nor pious?**

Every human being has a purpose; find your purpose and work towards your goals. A person with no purpose or goal in life receives no respect. He is a burden to others.

Cow that does not give milk nor conceives

What use is a cow if it neither gives milk nor produces calves? Milk can be either consumed or sold; either way, it is useful. A pregnant cow is also useful because it will give birth to a calf, which will become productive in the future. A cow which doesn't perform either of these functions is worthless.

Son who is neither learned nor pious

Similarly, what use is a poorly-educated son? An educated son can get a job and earn money. He is capable of looking after himself and his family. His achievements will make his parents proud. A pious son is an asset to the family. Through his good deeds he will uphold the family's honour. A son who is neither educated nor God-fearing is a disgrace to his family. He is a burden to his parents and siblings.

9.9

A short-lived son is better
Than a foolish son with long life
For the dead is mourned for a while
But the latter is a life-long sorrow

Which one would you prefer? A child with a short life span who makes you happy or an offspring with a long life who makes you miserable daily?

A short-lived son

It doesn't matter how long you live but how you live. Here Chanakya says a son who dies young is better compared to a dim-witted son with a long life. A fool brings disgrace to his parents through his actions. Everyone likes to have children. But the character of the children matters. What's the point of having a dunce for a son who is a constant source of pain and embarrassment?

Dead is mourned for a while

Chanakya is telling us the bitter truth here. He says it's better to have a child with a short life span than a simpleton for a son who lives long. Because, when a son dies, he's mourned for a short while. As they say, time is a great healer. You move on from great losses. But an dull-witted offspring will cause you sorrow for as long as he lives.

9.10

**Residing in an ill-reputed village,
Serving a low-life,
Unhealthy food, ill-tempered wife,
A foolish son and a widowed daughter
These six burn a person without fire**

An external fire can cause burn marks on the body or even burn a victim to death. However, sorrow is that fire that burns within a person. An internal fire leaves scars that never heal, nor are they noticeable.

Residence, service and food

Staying in an infamous village is stressful. It can tarnish one's good name because society associates the reputation of the residents with the reputation of the place where they live. And serving a scoundrel is no walk in the park; since he is incompetent, his management will make things difficult for his employees. Eating unhealthy food will harm your immune system because it doesn't provide nutrition to your body. Instead, it causes all sorts of diseases, be it high blood pressure, high cholesterol, diabetes, etc.

Wife, son and daughter

A wife who is ill-tempered destroys the peace in the house. And a son who is inefficient is no help to his family. A widowed daughter is always a worry for her parents because they don't want her to be lonely all her life. Parents are happy only when their children are

happy. All the above are enough reasons to make one burn with
worry.

9.11

The one attached to home can't learn
The one who eats meat has no compassion
The one who is greedy can't be truthful
The one who is devoted to women has no morality

Attachment leads to dependency. It also impairs logical thinking.
Certain ties hinder growth and turn one into a slave.

Home and meat-eater

Being overly attached to one's family and family life may hinder a
person's quest for knowledge. They say travel widens one's mind
but people who are attached to their family can't take off whenever
they please. The best type of education is gained from people and
places, not from books. So a family man is forced to put the needs
of his family first and keep his thirst for knowledge on the back
burner. According to Chanakya, meat-eaters have no compassion.
The reasoning behind his opinion could be that people who follow
a non-vegetarian diet consume the meat of animals slaughtered for
the sole purpose of filling their stomachs.

Greed and morality

A greedy person will go to any extent to make money. He will not
hesitate to use unethical means to earn money. In addition, a person
who is a slave to his sexual desires, and is devoted to the company
of women, has no morality. He will not think twice before chasing
a woman he desires.

9.12

A debt-incurring father is one's enemy
A mother fallen from virtue is one's enemy
A beautiful wife is one's enemy
And an unwise son is one's enemy

What are the real liabilities in life? Relatives who are dubious and untrustworthy can be a heavy burden. They say blood is thicker than water, but what if that blood is poisoned?

Father and mother

A father is expected to provide for the family and look after the interest of his children. But what about a father who accumulates only debts? He is his children's enemy, says Chanakya, because ultimately his children will have to pay off the family debt for no fault of their own. Likewise, a mother who is immoral is also her children's enemy. An adulteress is no role model for her children. Kids look up to their parents for guidance. Those parents who are unable to direct their offspring to live ethical lives will destroy their children's future. Such parents are worse than enemies.

Wife and son

If one has a beautiful wife that too is a problem. The wife attracting too much attention from other men could make the husband jealous and disturb his peace of mind. Thus a beautiful wife becomes a liability for the husband. And a dim-witted son becomes the parents' enemy as he brings a bad reputation to the family.

9.13

Separation from one's love, insult by one's kin,
An outstanding debt, service to a wicked king,
Impoverishment and attending a gathering of people
above one's stature
These can cause the heart to burn without fire

There are events and occasions in life where we experience only deep sorrow. And these incidents leave us scarred for life. Chanakya gives examples of such events.

Separation, insult and debt

Separation from your beloved is painful. A broken heart takes ages to heal. Also, insults from loved ones hurt the most. This could be because you care a lot about what they think about you. Debt is also a constant heartache and headache. You could lose all your wealth and even your dignity when the debt collectors turn up at your door step.

Service and gatherings

Serving an incompetent boss is never easy; it is stress-inducing, and therefore bad for physical and mental wellbeing. Obeying the instructions of unethical people is hell on earth if you are morally upright. Another unpleasant thing to do is attend a social gathering of people who are above your status. It is easy to feel out of place and uncomfortable in such circumstances. These six scenarios can cause a man to "burn" internally.

9.14

One who obstructs other people's work,
Is arrogant, selfish,
Deceitful, hateful and spiteful though soft-spoken
Such a Brahmin is cat-like

When intelligent people indulge in wrongdoings, they can be compared to a cat, says the master strategist.

The one who obstructs, is arrogant, selfish and deceitful

Smart people may use their intelligence for the wrong reasons. They can strategically obstruct some good work. They could be arrogant about the power. They could be very selfish and deceitful by nature.

Hateful and spiteful

Astute people could also turn spiteful. Don't be fooled by their soft-speech. A wise enemy is the most dangerous kind of enemy. Here Chanakya compares wise men who behave in this way to cats. They turn "catty" when they're annoyed.

9.15

The one who steals the belongings of the gods
and the guru,
Touches the wife of another,
And lives on other people's money
Such a Brahmin is a *Chandala*

Even a high-born Brahmin can behave in the most horrendous way. He could undertake activities that will bring shame upon his fellow beings. Such a Brahmin is no longer considered a high-born. He belongs to the lowest of the low classes.

Stealing and coveting

The one who robs the statues of deities and his teacher is despicable. Gods and teachers are revered in our culture. So a man who steals from them is loathsome. Likewise, a man who covets another's wife is detestable. According to Chanakya, another man's wife should be treated like one's own mother.

Chandala

A man who is dependent on others earns no respect. A man should be independent and not a burden to others. Like the rest of the men described above, such a parasite of a man is not a Brahmin but a *Chandala*, the lowest of the classes, says Chanakya.

9.16

**Even a pundit becomes grief-stricken
Giving sermons to a fool
Having a wicked wife
And being with the miserable**

Some people are so miserable and far-gone that even a wise person can't help them. It is useless to waste one's time on such hopeless cases.

Fools and wicked wives

What is the point of teaching a fool? It will only frustrate and infuriate the teacher. The student will remain ignorant, because he doesn't have the intellectual ability to comprehend what is being taught. Likewise, being married to a wicked woman is hopeless because she will not change her ways. The husband will ultimately feel self-pity for having such a wife.

Miserable company

Misery loves company and the miserable love to spread their despair. Pessimists upset the morale of anyone listening to them. Surround yourself with positive people and you'll be happy too. Positivity breeds positivity, so choose your friends wisely. A man who encounters a fool, has a wicked wife and miserable friends will fall prey to hopelessness.

9.17

**The beggar is a miser's enemy
The wise man is a fool's enemy
The husband is the wayward wife's enemy
And the moon is the enemy of the thief**

Some things just don't go together, like oil and water. Know what is good for you and avoid what can raze you to the ground.

The beggar and the wise man

A miser loves his money; he loathes parting with it. He also believes that one must earn one's keep. So a beggar, who asks for alms from others without doing any work, is a miser's adversary. A scholar is a fool's enemy because the former is intelligent and enjoys a higher status in society than the latter.

The husband and the moon

A disloyal wife considers her husband her enemy because he is a hindrance to her seeking pleasure elsewhere. A moonlit night is a thief's death trap because it exposes his misdeeds. As a result, he despises the moon.

9.18

**An indignant wife, a deceitful friend,
An offending servant,
And the snake-inhabited house
Are no doubt death warrants**

Be careful of all those around you, warns Chanakya. Know whom to trust and whom not to, even if people seem to care about you. They can be wicked in their ways.

Wife and friend

A discontented wife will always demand something or the other. Her malcontent will cause her husband significant stress. And if one's friend turns out to be disloyal, one will be devastated.

Living with snakes

A house is not fit for human inhabitation if there are reptiles around. Who wants to live with snakes! Poisonous or not, one is unaccustomed to live in such an environment. Through these examples, Chanakya advises us to be constantly alert and ensure that we don't unwittingly get into harmful, even fatal, situations.

9.19

**Death of the wife in old age
Wealth gone into the hands of kin
Dependence on others for food
These three are mortifying for men**

Self-respecting individuals don't depend on others for their survival. When circumstances force such people to ask for help, they feel ashamed.

Death of the wife and wealth in others' hand

As most people age, their friend circle reduces and they depend more on their spouses for company. A man's wife becomes his most trusted friend as they age. If an aged man loses his wife, he will feel terribly lonely. When one's hard-earned wealth is lost to one's relatives, one is left devastated.

Depending on others for food

Food is a basic necessity. As an adult, not being financially independent, even to buy one's own food, makes one feel insignificant. It hurts the ego and dents one's confidence. The three situations discussed above are humiliating, says Chanakya.

9.20

Those who disclose
Secrets of others are evil
They meet their downfall
As a snake who strays into anthills

Those who betray the trust of others are dishonourable. Such vile and manipulative people eventually will meet a dire fate.

Disclosing secrets

Every man considers his secret sacred; he keeps it close to his heart and guards it from the prying outside world. If someone shares his secret with you, he trusts you. If you were to reveal this secret information to a third party, it would be a gross betrayal of trust. Trust once lost is not easy to restore.

Snake in an anthill

People who disclose others' secrets will meet with their downfall like the snake that strays into anthills unknowingly. The ants will attack the snake, eventually killing it. The snake will have no chance to escape. Likewise, malicious gossipmongers will get ambushed one day when they least expect it, predicts Chanakya.

9.21

Meat-eaters, drunkards,
Fools and illiterates
Are beasts in human form
And add to the earth's burden

Chanakya's school of thought considers some people worse than animals. They simply add to the world's woes.

Meat-eaters and drunkards

According to Chanakya, eating animal flesh (even though it is cooked), is crude; in his days most upper-class people were vegetarians. He considers killing animals and eating their meat barbarian. Drunkards are addicted to alcohol, so they don't use their intelligence and waste away their God-given life. Under the influence, they indulge in immoral activities and create chaos in society.

Fools and illiterates

Like alcoholics, fools too don't use their brains. They don't live up to their full human potential. So according to Chanakya, such people cannot be considered human beings but animals. They don't use their superior intellect, the key faculty that separates men from beasts. Such people are a burden on mother earth, says Chanakya.

9.22

Between a scoundrel and a snake
The snake is better
For the snake strikes only when provoked
But the scoundrel does it at every turn

A depraved person is more dangerous than a venomous snake. The snake will bite only when it feels threatened, but an evil person will try to harm you every chance he gets.

A scoundrel and a snake

No one can predict what is in the mind of a scoundrel. He is more venomous than a serpent, according to Chanakya. Everybody is scared of serpents because of their potentially dangerous bite. However, it is difficult to tell how dangerous an evil-minded person could be. How do you know which person is dangerous and which one is not? That too is a dilemma.

Scoundrels worse than snakes

There is a saying that human beings are more dangerous than animals. While animals kill to eat or to protect themselves, humans are capable of killing without any need whatsoever. A snake strikes to protect itself, but a scoundrel strikes as and when he pleases.

9.23

Laziness ruins knowledge
Money is lost when entrusted with others
A farmland is wasted without seeds
And an army is lost without a commander

Do what is required of you and you shall prosper or else ruin will head your way, warns Chanakya through this *neeti*.

Laziness and money

A lazy person wastes his skills and knowledge. Only if you put in the effort will you find success. Your knowledge is useful only if you are able to apply it to real life situations. And when you entrust your money to others, it is lost. So be very careful when you part with your wealth.

Seeds and a commander

What is the use of farmland if there are no seeds to be sown? It will become barren and unproductive. Likewise, an army is useless if there is no commander to guide it. Soldiers require a leader to give them instructions; they are used to following orders. Without a head, an army soon plunges into disorder.

9.24

**Trees on a river bank
A woman in another man's house
A king without advisors
Without doubt go quickly to ruin**

You get into trouble if you are at the wrong place at the wrong time. Certain circumstances are toxic to your existence; know what is good for you and what is not and act accordingly. To succeed in life, you need to know what kind of environment suits you best.

Trees and women

If you notice, trees on river banks don't last long. They get uprooted during floods and get washed away. A woman who lives-in with a man who is not her husband will find herself in trouble. Our society has not progressed enough to accommodate single men and women living together without frowning upon them. So Chanakya says such a woman will invite problems her way sooner or later.

King without counsellors

A king requires counsel on running his kingdom. Without guidance from his ministers and guru, his downfall is certain. If the king wants to have a long, stable reign, he should have a council of ministers to guide him on every matter.

9.25

How can people be happy with a corrupt ruler?
How can one fall back on a friend who is insincere?
How can the family be happy with a discordant spouse?
How can one gain glory by teaching an undisciplined pupil?

Happiness depends on various factors. Chanakya gives four examples here that demonstrate how certain human equations don't work.

Corrupt leader and insincere friend

How can one be happy under a corrupt leader? People's needs won't be taken care of under such a leader. Corruption leads to chaos and disharmony. And how can one fall back on a friend who is not dependable? A friend is someone who can be relied on during tough times. An insincere person who is close to you is your enemy, not someone worthy of your friendship.

Discordant spouse and undisciplined pupil

A couple in an acrimonious relationship turn a home into hell. An unpleasant spouse can make life difficult for the partner. Also, if a student is undisciplined and unworthy, how can his teacher gain glory at all? A good student excels with the right guidance. But a bad one can't be helped even if the teacher spoon-feeds him wisdom. Such a pupil will only bring bad reputation to his teacher.

9.26

O jackal, leave alone that body at once
Whose hands that never gave any alms
Whose ears that never heard any holy discourses
Whose eyes never saw the sight of sages
Whose feet that were not used for pilgrimages
Whose stomach was fed with ill-gotten money
Whose head was kept erect with vain glory
Do not eat that body
Otherwise, you will become polluted

We have been blessed with a body which has unlimited potential. But the real beauty of the human body is in the activities it performs. To honour the God-given gift of this physique, Chanakya advises us to use one's whole body to serve others.

Hands, ears and eyes

The hands are to be used for charity. The ears are meant for listening to holy discourses and inspiring tales about the lives of great men, women and sages. The eyes should look towards wise men for guidance.

Feet, stomach and head

The feet should be used for pilgrimages. The stomach should never be satisfied with food that is bought with money earned unethically. And the head should not be held high in vanity. A man who has not followed these suggestions is defiled. Even his dead body is not fit for animal consumption.

9.27

On gaining wealth, who hasn't felt proud?
Who has put an end to his miseries?
Whose heart has not been broken by a woman?
Who, indeed, is always a favourite of the sovereign?
Who hasn't fallen prey to death?
Which beggar has gained respect?
Fallen into the trap of bad company
Who has traversed the path of milk and honey?

Nothing in this world is flawless or easy. Everything comes at a price and sometimes you have to go with the flow.

Wealth, miseries and broken hearts

When someone becomes successful and wealthy, he feels a sense of pride. It is only natural. That is why charity is recommended for the rich. Give what you have in abundance to those who have none of it. In this way you will appreciate what you have all the more. No one lives a consistently happy life. Life comes with its challenges and struggles, and that is its beauty. Heartbreak is also a part of life. If you need love, you must also be prepared for heartbreak. There is no way you can experience one without the other.

Sovereign, death, beggar and bad company

A king changes his mind from time to time; his likes and dislikes too change accordingly. So no one can remain a king's favourite for long. Men are mortals; we all die one day. This is the reality of life. And a beggar gets no respect because he depends on others to survive. Only hard work is respected in society. Stay away from bad company because once you've fallen into that trap, you won't be able to tell good and bad apart. The path to heaven (here Chanakya refers to heaven as "the land of milk and honey") is only for the righteous.

9.28

The Brahmin who is indifferent to the destruction of
A tank, a well, a lake, a garden,
And a holy place
Is a barbarian

A wise person should not support vandalism. If he does, he is a barbarous person indeed. He should instead help the society he is a part of in any way he can.

A tank, well, lake and garden

Any source of clear drinking water is sacred. Water is the source of life. The absence of water means death. The world over people struggle to find clean drinking water. Some regions of the world suffer terribly under draught. At the same time, a well-kept garden is a source of beauty and a sight to behold!

Their destruction

A wise person shouldn't be the one to keeps quite about the destruction of these water resources, gardens and holy places. He should be cognizant of their immeasurable value. Anyone who ruins them is indeed an uncivilized brute, and a wise man who supports such an act is no better either.

9.29

As one dried-up tree
Makes the whole forest burn
So is the distress caused to the whole family
By a wicked son

One bad member can destroy an entire family. Here Chanakya uses the example of forest fire to make his point.

Dried-up tree

Most wild fires start very small. A single dry tree can cause forest fires that rage on for days, spreading for acres and destroying everything on their path.

Wicked son

Similarly, the sorrow caused by a wicked son can adversely affect all family members. It takes just one bad offspring to tarnish a family's reputation, and once destroyed, it cannot be regained. So be conscious of the consequences of your actions, especially their impact on your loved ones.

CHAPTER 10

DOs

10.1

Generosity, austerity, courage,
Knowledge, politeness and wisdom
Don't have airs about having these
For the earth has many gems (with such qualities)

People who have the qualities mentioned above are considered gems in this world. However, if you possess these qualities, don't be arrogant, because there are many others like you as well, cautions Chanakya.

Generosity, austerity and courage

Generosity is the willingness to help others without expecting anything in return. Austerity is the way of simple living, without any material comforts. And courage is the strength to carry on in spite of danger.

Knowledge, politeness and wisdom

Knowledge is the virtue of distinguished men. They are sought after for their wisdom. People who are knowledgeable are usually polite and humble. One should not be haughty about possessing all of these qualities because there are many others who have these qualities too.

10.2

Till this body is healthy
And death is distant
Perform the deeds beneficial to the soul
When death is at the door, what can you do?

Nobody is immortal; death is inevitable and will arrive one day without notice. But the good news is that one can perform good deeds before it is too late.

Healthy body

Till this body is healthy, everything is good. However, this condition won't last long. The body suffers wear and tear over the course of time. Once the body starts ageing, you will face many health issues and won't be able to function as you would like to; you may even need help to go about your day. The younger and healthier you are, the better it is for you. Be aware of the fact that one day you will weaken and die. Do what you have to do before that day comes.

Perform good deeds

When you are healthy, you don't need anyone's assistance to go around helping others and performing good deeds. As you age, it will become difficult to even move from one room to the other. And when you are on your deathbed, what's the point in regretting wasted time? So don't delay your plans to do charitable deeds you feel strongly about. Doing good to others helps your soul. According to Hindu thought, you will be collecting *punya* by doing such deeds. Time is precious. Before you know it, the years will fly by and the young you will be a grandmother or grandfather struggling to catch up with your grandchildren.

10.3

Nectar can be extracted even from poison
Gold can be picked up from filth
Knowledge can be acquired even from a low-born
And a girl can be virtuous even if born in a family
of ill-repute

Don't judge a book by its cover. A commoner could be extremely polite while an upper-class individual could behave like a ruffian; people's backgrounds may or may not have an effect on their bearing. So don't be too quick to judge.

Nectar from poison and gold from filth

When gods and demons came together to churn the Ocean of Milk for *amrit*, the elixir of immortality, they first extracted *kalakooda* or *Halahala*, the lethal poison that Lord Shiva drank to protect the universe from annihilation. They were able to extract *amrit* only after that. Gold is mined from rock and dirt in mines. Despite its origins, gold is still precious.

Knowledge from a low-born and a girl from ill-reputed family

Knowledge doesn't discriminate. One can acquire knowledge even from a low-born if he is qualified to teach. Likewise, a girl could be from a disreputable family but still be virtuous. Don't evaluate people based on their family status, as you could be in for a surprise.

10.4

Let not a single day go by
Without learning a hymn, half of it or a quarter,
Or even a word of it,
Nor performing charity, study or prescribed work

Don't waste a single day, says Chanakya. Your days on earth are limited, so use them wisely. Attend to your duties. Make your days count.

Hymns

Prayers help one get through the days even when some days are tedious. Prayers nourish the soul, so learn or recite a holy verse every day. Even if you can't recite a full verse, do recite half of it. If that's not possible, recite a quarter of the verse. Even a word from a single verse will do, says Chanakya. These sacred hymns have the power to cleanse a person. Therefore, don't end a day without saying a short prayer.

Charity, study and prescribed work

If possible, do something good and charitable, every day. It is not necessary that your good deed should be a magnanimous gesture; even getting a tired colleague a cup of coffee without being asked to is a good deed. Also, try to learn something every day. This will help you in the future and reward you when you least expect it. Finish the job that was assigned to you that day itself; don't leave it for tomorrow. Who knows about tomorrow? By doing all the listed activities here, you are making sure every single day of yours is productive and will eventually lead to a fulfilling life.

10.5

Sugarcane, water, milk, radish,
Betel leaf, fruits and herbal remedies
Even after consuming these
Bathing and benefaction be done as usual

Indians place a lot of emphasis on cleanliness—keeping clean by bathing on a daily basis is an important part of an individual's routine. No matter what you consume, even if it is good for your health, don't skip your daily ablutions.

Sugarcane, water, milk and radish

We have always been told that one needs to cleanse one's mouth after eating. Sugarcane can leave little particles in one's mouth. Wash it away with water. Even if you drink milk, which is nutritious, clean your mouth. Radish can leave a strong odour, so brush your teeth thoroughly after relishing radish-based dishes.

Betel leaf, fruits and herbal medicines

It is customary in India to chew betel leaves as a mouth freshner after a meal. But then do brush your teeth after that. Do the same after consuming fruits. Fruits do contain natural sugar and one needs to get rid of any sugar residue as soon as possible to protect one's teeth. Herbal medicines can also stain your mouth and tarnish your teeth. So cleanse well after consuming such medicines.

10.6

All charities and sacrifices performed for gain
Will only bring temporary results
But gifts given to the deserving
And protection offered to all beings shall never perish

Never help anyone expecting something in return. Also, never take credit for your kind gestures. If you do, there is no merit in your charity.

Charity and sacrifices performed for gain

A noble deed is done with a selfless spirit, expecting nothing in return, not even an ego boost. When you give away something, with an aim to get something back, even if it is just praise or a pat on the back, it doesn't count as charity.

Gifting those who are deserving

A selfless act of helping someone in dire need or protecting someone from harm will earn you merit, even if you don't expect it. Your rewards will come in the most unexpected manner. The deserving will surely reap the benefits of their good work.

10.7

An action contemplated in the mind
Shouldn't be advertised
But keep it a secret like a mantra
And reveal it in time

The success of Chanakya lay in the secrecy he employed in everything he did. Here he advises us not to reveal our secrets until the appropriate time. Like a sacred mantra, keep it only to yourself.

Do not advertise your plans

An action plan or project that you have in mind should not be shared with others prematurely. The moment you let the cat out of the bag, it's no longer just your idea. There are risks associated with exposing an idea to the world in a half-baked stage. Some might even try to jeopardize your plan without understanding your idea fully. Therefore, anything you have in your mind should be announced in public only at the right time.

Announce projects only in time

Wait till your plan has taken complete shape before announce it to the world. Keep your unrealised plans close to your heart, like a secret mantra. In our culture, the significance of a mantra is very high. Only a guru will pass it on to his student, and that too after many years of study. Such a sacred mantra is not supposed to be shared with anybody else.

10.8

Be satisfied with these three:
Your own wife, food and money
And relent not with these three:
Study, meditation and charity

Know what to be satisfied with and what not to compromise. Only when this balance is achieved can a person live a fulfilling life. In this *neeti*, Chanakya shows you which is which.

One's own wife, food and money

Be happy with your own spouse. A marriage takes work, so if you feel your married life is not as rosy as you would like it to be, work on it instead of looking for pleasure and distraction elsewhere. Food is considered sacred in India. As a result we celebrate many harvest festivals. One should be satisfied with a moderate diet and not be a glutton. And also, be satisfied with the money that you have earned ethically. Don't be greedy; don't try to amass wealth through illegal or immoral means.

Study, meditation and charity

Albert Einstein is thought to have said, "Once you stop learning you start dying." You should never give up on learning something new every day. It will enrich you and help you live a better quality life. Without the curiosity and eagerness to learn something new, life becomes boring. Meditate every day too. Give some time to yourself to quieten your mind. This will help you de-clutter your head and relax. Only a calm mind can scale heights. And finally, always be altruistic. Help out those who have nothing with what little you have. It will bring you, more lasting peace and happiness than if you had bought the latest smartphone or an expensive car for yourself.

10.9

**Penance should be done alone
Study by two and singing by three
A journey should be undertaken by four,
Agriculture by five
And battle by an army**

Certain things are better done alone while others are better conducted in a group. You need to understand which ones to do on your own and which ones to do with other people.

Penance, study and singing

Penance and atonement is a personal journey. No one else can undertake them for you. Therefore, you need to do penance in private. On the other hand, when it comes to studying, especially revising, it is better to do it with a friend or fellow student with whom you can discuss the subject and clear your doubts. Likewise, three people singing together in harmony is a marvelous treat.

Journey, agriculture and battle

According to Chanakya, four people make an ideal travel team. It is easy to pair up this way too, which is always helpful in long journeys. So with four people, you are not alone, or stuck with just one person. Neither is your group too big to handle. If it is farming you have in mind, Chanakya recommends having five people to do the labour. And in a battle, better be ready with many men. An army is required to fight a war; one cannot go into a battlefield alone and expect to win.

10.10

**It's the giving of gifts that makes the hands gracious,
Not the bracelet
It's the act of taking a bath that cleanses the body,
Not the sandalwood paste
It's the act of giving respect that gives satisfaction,
Not refreshments
It's the knowledge that brings salvation,
Not self-adornment**

One should know how to discern between the fake and real. He who knows this is an intelligent person. Therefore, develop the quality of refined judgment.

Gifts and bath

The beauty of one's hands is not in the ornaments one wears. They are only embellishments. The hands that do charity are the most beautiful hands. And it is not the sandalwood paste that one applies to the face that cleans the body, but the bath one takes before applying the paste.

Respect and knowledge

When you are respectful towards other people, you feel satisfied with yourself. And no refreshments in the world can give you that kind of satisfaction. Also, it is knowledge that protects the soul from ruination, not ornaments or decorations.

10.11

**He who sheds shyness when dealing with money
In acquiring knowledge
In eating and in business
Gains satisfaction**

You must be bold to state what you want, only then will you get it. Never shy away from claiming what is rightfully yours. The world doesn't care about those who keep quiet out of inhibition.

Money and knowledge

People often feel awkward when talking about money, especially the money they are owed. Speak freely and frankly to your debtor; make him aware that he needs to pay you back. If you don't ask for your own money, no one else will do it for you. The same goes for salary hikes. Don't be shy. Ask for a raise if you feel you qualify for one. If you don't state your case to your superior, you will be overlooked during annual salary appraisals. Also, don't feel self-conscious to broaden your horizons through education. Knowledge is for all and there is no age limit to learning. You can start to learn something new whenever you apply your mind to it.

Food and business

If you want to go for a second helping during a meal, just go for it. No man should feel shy or guilty about eating. It is better to satisfy your stomach than go hungry. Shyness is not profitable in business either; a shy businessman will never rake in profits. In business, one needs to be bold to generate sales. A businessman is also a leader; he often needs to make strong and sometimes unpopular decisions and stick to them. He has a huge responsibility on his shoulders. Shying away from those responsibilities will not help.

10.12

He who is content with a single meal
Who performs the sixteen samskaras
Who only sleeps with his wife when she is well
Is a true Brahmin

A true Brahmin is the one who is content with less in life, who is dutiful and mindful, says Chanakya. Such a person is a noble and realised soul.

A single meal and 16 purification rituals

Though Chanakya encourages us to eat well, he also reminds us that overeating is not healthy. A wise man should be aware of the dangers of gluttony. Our forefathers survived on one or two meals a day. Today, with all our "nutritious diets," we suffer from more lifestyle-related illnesses than they did. Another practice Chanakya advises for a wise man is the 16 *samskaras* (rituals). The Vedic scriptures list these rituals to be performed by a Brahmin. Only he who performs these rituals without fail is a true Brahmin, says Chanakya.

Wife in good health

Chanakya goes on to state that a true Brahmin is also one who cares for his wife's wellbeing. He enjoys conjugal relations with her only when she is in good health. Respecting one's wife is paramount in Indian culture; giving her support and help when she is ill is a husband's duty.

10.13

**Marry your daughter into a good family
Give your son the best education
Bind the enemy with vices
And engage with righteous friends**

Know what to fit where. Happiness can be achieved with the right pairing of people and things. Here are some examples of good associations.

Daughter and son

In India, it is the responsibility of the parents to make sure that their daughter is married into a good family. She should be safe and treated well in her new home. Likewise, Chanakya says a son should be paired with good education, since it was a son's duty to look after his old parents during Chanakya's time. His education should also help him develop a strong character.

Enemy and friends

Even though it is not wise to incite people, Chanakya advises us to make sure one deals with one's enemy if necessary and make him suffer for his wrongdoings. Be careful about who you hang out with; pair yourself with good people. Righteous friends will not lead you astray or lead you into any trouble.

10.14

**Wise men bring up their children
To be virtuous
For those children who are well-behaved and ethical
Bring glory upon their families**

Teach your children to be exemplary human beings. Those who are wise pay attention to their children's behaviour and teach them to be principled individuals. Children are the future; teach them how to be model citizens from the time they are young.

Children of wise people

Children are like sponges; they absorb whatever they see and hear quickly. Intelligent parents know this and teach their offspring to be honest and ethical as early as possible.

Bring glory to the family

Children who are upstanding are appreciated and loved by all. Everyone will speak highly about polite kids. Such children represent their parents' upbringing, and well-bought up kids invariably bring praise to their parents and family.

10.15

O I flower! Though you are a resort for snakes
Fruitless, prickly and crooked
You thrive in the mud; not easily approachable
Yet with your fragrance you fascinate everyone!
Indeed, one merit overcomes every other imperfection

One good quality can cover up many imperfections. Chanakya gives the example of *ketki* flower here to drive home the point. Its fragrance compensates for its many other imperfections.

The problems

The *ketki* flower is a very common bloom that finds mention in Indian literature. The flower of the pandanus or screwpine tree/ shrub, it is highly fragrant. As a result, it's even used in making perfumes and essential oils. However, the tree is home for poisonous snakes, Chanakya says. This particular tree doesn't bear edible fruits and is covered in thorns. It is also crooked in shape. It is not easy to approach the tree because it grows in the mud near riverbanks.

The advantage

However, the most noteworthy quality of the flower is its fragrance. It is sweet and captivating, indeed. With its smell, the *ketki* flower attracts everyone. Therefore, Chanakya says, one merit compensates all its other demerits. So be like the *ketki* flower and cultivate a brilliant quality even though you have many imperfections.

10.16

Reconcile with the stronger
Counter the weaker
Deal with the enemy equal in strength
With politeness or force as may be proper

Know who your enemy is and what his strengths and weaknesses are. Prepare a plan to either defeat the enemy or befriend him. This *neeti* is among the most famous strategies of Chanakya. Another version of *'sama, dana, danda, bheda,'* this *neeti* advises us to counter people of different sorts in the way that befit them.

Stronger and weaker enemies

When someone is stronger than you, it is useless to fight him. Instead, it is better to reconcile with him. Haven't you heard the saying, 'keep you friends close and enemies closer'? But if your enemy is weaker than you, you can go into attack mode.

Politeness or force

With an enemy who is your equal, you can either use politeness or force, depending upon what type of a person your adversary is. If he is a polite person, you can use politeness to smooth over the ruffled edges. But if he is a brute, then use force, says Chanakya. The real strategy is in deciding what works for which person. One size does not fit all. So you need to be intelligent enough to use the right method to get the best outcome in tricky situations.

10.17

Restrain an elephant with a goad
A horse with a harness
Restrain a horned animal with a stick
And a scoundrel with a sword

How to control someone depends on what type of a person he is. Each animal is controlled using special equipment that fits only their kind. Have you ever seen an elephant on a leash? No, leashes are for dogs. Likewise, you can keep people in check by knowing what their individual soft spots are.

Elephant and horse

The elephant is a huge animal, many times bigger and stronger than a human being. If the elephant is domesticated, one can control him using a thin goad without much difficulty. A horse is energetic and full of vigour; it likes to run around and play. But using a harness, a wild horse can be tamed and used to do your bidding.

Horned animal and a scoundrel

Horned animals like the cow and buffalo are controlled with a stick. A shepherd can easily manage a herd of cows using a single staff. Likewise, a scoundrel can also be brought to his senses—by using a sword. Here Chanakya says treat people how they deserve to be treated. A man with no principles should be restrained using harsh methods; no gentle manners will do for such a person.

10.18

Keep a distance of five *hastas* from a carriage
Ten *hastas* from a war horse
A thousand *hastas* from the elephant
And quit the place of the villainous

Be aware of your surroundings and the people you mix with. If you are naïve about the circumstances you are in, you will suffer losses, cautions Chanakya.

Keep a distance

It's best to keep a distance of five *hastas* (a traditional Indian unit of length, measured from the elbow to the tip of the middle finger) from a carriage because in the olden days horses used to draw the carriages and they could stop and lift their tail without notice. Anyone standing nearby is sure to be splashed with the beast's dung or urine. It's best to keep your distance from a war horse too (10 *hastas*). Horses used in wars are usually highly strung since they are in the middle of action throughout. They get annoyed easily, so it's best to not be too close to such an animal.

Avoid the villainous

A virtuous person spending time with a wicked one is like pure drinking water getting mixed with sewage water. Evil people don't feel remorse while engaging in illegal or immoral activities. They are selfish and will always look for opportunities to get ahead, even if that means hurting somebody else in the process. So be careful with such people; any association with them will only end in your ruin.

10.19

**Sugarcane, sesame seed, a lazy person,
An amorous woman, gold and earth,
Sandalwood, curd and betel leaf:
Rubbing improves their worth**

It is important to know how to get the best out of a situation. Here is a list of a few things whose worth can be assessed by rubbing and crushing them.

Sugarcane, sesame seed and a lazy person

Sugarcane is crushed for its juice. After processing its stalk, it produces sugar. It's sweetness is revealed only after it is crushed. Sesame seeds produce oil if you crush them. Likewise, a lazy person needs to be pushed hard to get the best work out of him, says Chanakya.

Amorous women, gold, earth, sandalwood, curd and betel leaf

Chanakya says amorous women should be loved. Gold shines when polished. Earth becomes fertile when ploughed and sandalwood produces fragrant paste when rubbed with stone. Ghee or clarified butter is obtained by treating curd, and betel leaf is enjoyed by chewing it with some areca nuts. All these items improve in quality after being rubbed. Therefore, understand what works for a person and treat him accordingly to produce great results.

10.20

The student, the servant, the traveller,
The hungry, the frightened,
The storekeeper and the watchman,
These seven should be awakened if fallen asleep

People in certain situations need to be always alert; they cannot
afford to fall asleep as and when they wish. Chanakya lists seven
such categories of people who need to be woken up if they fall
asleep.

The student, servant and traveller

A student is supposed to be studying or reading most of the time.
If he falls asleep in the class, it doesn't help him in acquiring
knowledge or good grades. A servant should be awake and alert
while his employer is awake; he doesn't get to enjoy the luxury of
sleep whenever he finds a chance. A traveller cannot afford to fall
asleep on his way because he could be in unfamiliar terrain. He may
lose his way or encounter dangerous elements.

The hungry, the frightened, the storekeeper and the watchman

A hungry person should not be allowed to fall asleep on an empty
stomach. One must feed him, even if he has to be woken up from
sleep. A frightened person shouldn't be allowed to nod off without
alleviating his fears because he will be haunted by nightmares. The
storekeeper should take vigilant care of his store or else he may be
robbed. The the watchman is expected to gaurd the property he is
stationed at. If these seven people are found sleeping, wake them
up immediately, says Chanakya.

10.21

He who eats his meals silently
For one full year
Will live for many years
With complete happiness

Silence is golden. And here Chanakya suggests a practical way for observing silence through which one can attain heavenly bliss in life.

Silent meals

Many of us feel that mealtimes are for bonding and sharing with friends and family. Chanakya has a different outlook; he believes that one must observe silence while eating. Use this time to thank God for providing a good meal and meditate upon him. He advises us to do this for one full year. That is quite difficult, no doubt. But when it develops into a habit, it will come to you naturally.

Happiness

Mealtimes are one of those occasions during which a person can focus on himself and even contemplate. Doing this daily, at every meal, even if it is for just ten minutes, will prove beneficial. Try this and you will feel refreshed and stress-free after such a meal. When you are not stressed, you will naturally enjoy life more and feel blessed.

10.22

Give up a member to save a family
Give up the family to save a village
Give up a village for the country
And give up the world to save your soul!

Learn to prioritise. Nothing is important than yourself. Always keep that in mind, even if you have to sacrifice something very dear to save yourself. Here's how:

Family and village

According to Chanakya, if you have to sacrifice a family member to save your family, don't hesitate. For example, if you have an unlawful sibling, turn him in for the sake of the other members of the family. Or else the entire extended family will suffer the consequences. Likewise, when your village is in trouble, forsake your family and join the community to help others. For example, don't cling on to your own family if your village is engulfed in a fire; run out and save as many people as you can.

Village and world

A village is nothing in front of saving your own motherland. So if you have to desert your village to save your country, do so. But don't forget that above all, it is you who matters the most. So if you are in a situation where you have to escape the world to save your soul, do so, advises Chanakya.

CHAPTER 11

DON'Ts

11.1

Though chopped, the sandalwood tree does not lose its scent
Even when old, the elephant does not give up his sportiness
Though pressed in a machine, the sugarcane
does not lose its sweetness
The high-born, though impoverished, does not
forsake his gentleness

The basic nature of a person or an object does not change at all, even when his circumstances or surroundings change.

Sandalwood trees and elephants

Sandalwood trees retain their fragrance even when they are chopped down. Now let's take the case of elephants; they love to have fun in the wild, no matter how old they are. Be it playing in the mud or wandering through the forest looking for food, these giant animals know how to enjoy themselves, even when they get old.

Sugarcane and a high-born person

Sugarcane does not lose its sweetness even when it is crushed in a machine. And so is the case with noble people. Even in utter poverty, they will maintain their dignity and gentleness. The message here is, try to find your true self and hold on to it. Don't try to change according to the demands of the world. By being your authentic self, you will also attract people and opportunities that are more suited for yourself—a foolproof way to climb the success ladder.

11.2

At the time of a deluge
Oceans are known to exceed their boundaries
And seek to change
But a gentleman never changes, even during a
catastrophe

A person exhibits his real character when faced with a misfortune. Most people wear a mask of niceness and moral uprightness in their everyday life to be accepted and liked by society, but this mask comes off when real tragedy hits. Only those who are authentic don't change under stress.

The ocean during a deluge

During a storm, the ocean tends to overflow and cause damage to the shore. It creates havoc and destroys everything in its wake. At times, it could even change its trajectory forever. The flow of the water is unpredictable.

A gentleman in catastrophe

However, a gentleman under unfavourable circumstances is another matter altogether. He does not lose his mind; he remains calm and gentle as always. This shows strength of character. Only a true gent will be able to weather a storm and come out of it without his personality undergoing any change whatsoever. Strive to be a gentleman of such strong character; don't panic in the face of change, but face it with all your might.

11.3

At the end of a *yuga*, the Meru mountain may shake
At the end of a *kalpa*, all the seven seas may churn
But a sage will never
Veer from his path of righteousness

Chanakya says that everything in this world is temporary; only the
path of a sage is permanent.

Mount Meru and the seven seas

In Hindu mythology, Mount Meru is a sacred four-peaked mountain.
It is said to have been in existence for millennia. According to
Chanakya, even Meru may shake when a *yuga* (era) comes to an
end. The seven seas or the world's oceans may churn when a *kalpa*
(considered to be the length of a single cycle of the cosmos from
creation to dissolution) ends.

A sage will not waver

A sage who has acquired true wisdom will not waver from his path
of righteousness, come what may. His aim and determination to
find the truth will never be destroyed. This is the power of human
will. And faith in oneself is the ultimate strength. A wise man knows
this truth.

11.4

Spurning kinsmen is fatal
Offending others causes loss of money
Hostility towards the king triggers one's own downfall
But the scorn of a Brahmin brings ruin to the
whole family

Don't go looking for trouble. Treat people with the respect and
goodwill they deserve. Otherwise, things could turn fatal, warns
Chanakya.

Kinsmen and other people

Relatives are an integral part of family life; they provide support in
times of need. But spurning a well-wishing relative could be fatal.
You may even get ostracized by the extended family for ill-treating
a relative. Likewise, don't offend other people for no reason. You
could lose a lot of money. These days many people approach the
courts with lawsuits against others for minor reasons. Such disputes
are money-drainers, and even if you win ithe case, your coffers could
be bleeding by the time the final verdict is out.

King and Brahmin

The king is the most powerful person in his kingdom. Being hostile
to a ruler will only end in your downfall. He has all the means
to make your life miserable. So be careful when you argue with
authority figures. But of all the people you should not offend, a
wise man should be at the top of the list, because he could ruin
your entire family. Nothing can substitute intelligence and when
an intelligent man decides to come after you, stay out of his way.

11.5

Do not confide in the unfriendly
Nor trust an ordinary friend
For if he gets angry with you
All your secrets could be revealed

You must guard your secrets from everyone, even from close friends. Human temperament is unpredictable and you never know who decides to harm you and when. Here Chanakya advises us to never trust anyone with our secrets.

Unfriendly person and ordinary friend

Never share your secrets with unfriendly people, because they may use them against you. When you share a secret with another, you are giving power to that person to destroy you. Don't even trust a friend in the matters of secrets. Your secrets are something that should always remain with you alone.

Secrets revealed in anger

Not telling a secret to an unfriendly person is a matter of commonsense. But why not share it with a dear friend? Because no relationship is permanent. One never knows when a friend will become a foe. Anger or resentment can change a person. So if your friend gets angry with you and is looking for ways to hurt you, revealing your secrets to the world is the easiest way to do it. So keep your secrets close to your heart. Don't give anyone the power to hurt you.

11.6

A wise man should not reveal
His loss of money, agonies of his mind,
The misconduct of his wife,
Deception by others,
And insults spoken to him

A wise man should keep all his problems to himself. Revealing his troubles, as in the case of secrets, will also make him a soft target. There is no reason to broadcast your difficulties and worries to others. Share only what is necessary.

Loss of money and agonies

There will be many problems in your life. Dealing with challenges is a part of being an adult. Money troubles are the worst out of the lot. In a material world like ours, living without money is very difficult. Likewise, worries and anxieties are also a part of life. Nobody is always happy. But knowing that is the key. Don't overly share your worries because what you worry about says a lot about you.

Misconduct of the wife, deceptions and insults

If one's wife is not virtuous, that is a cause for grief. What transpires between couples in their relationship should be kept between themselves. Sharing your marital issues with others can prove harmful to your reputation. Likewise, if you were ever deceived or insulted, keep this information with you. It is not wise to talk about something unfortunate that happened to you, especially with those who are not very close to you. People may sympathise with you on your face but may mock you behind your back. No one deserves public mockery. Not many are sensitive to other's pain, so it is best to keep your troubles to yourself and remain calm.

11.7

**A wise man should not reveal the formula of a drug
he has prepared,
An act of charity he has performed,
Rifts in the family, private affairs with his wife,
Unrefined food he may have been offered,
Or scandalous talks he may have heard**

Smart people maintain confidentiality in their lives. They don't air their dirty laundry in public nor do they reveal their success secrets. Their private lives are kept private and their conduct is dignified.

Drug formula, charitable act and family discord

If you have a medical remedy, like a homemade potion that works, guard it, says Chanakya. In his days, such secrets were very valuable, because medicines were rare and people would do anything to get their hands on certain cures. In today's time, this will apply to your insights that help you being successful. Keep your success secrets close, otherwise bad elements may misuse them.

A noble person will never publicise his largesse. People who receive your help may be grateful to you, but they also don't want to feel small. That's what happens when a charitable act is made public. Also, all families have conflicts. They could be small or big. But it is not prudent to let the world know what's going on within your family. Good or bad, family matters are best contained within the the four walls of your house.

Private affairs, unrefined food and scandalous talk

The relationship between a man and his wife is a private matter to be kept between them. It shouldn't be discussed in public. It is disrespectful and in bad taste. Marriage is a pure and scared institution; it should be given due respect. If someone has offered you uncooked food, don't embarrass him by criticizing it. No one serves bad food intentionally. Take it as an oversight and forgive him for the blunder. It is hurtful for the host to hear his guests criticize the food served at his table. Do not be party to loose talk. If you ever happened to be in the midst of such conversation, politely excuse yourself and walk away. Wise people stay away from scandalous talk. No one benefits from such salacious conversations. They don't expand one's mind or impart wisdom.

11.8

One shouldn't be too upright
Go and see for yourself the forests
Where the straight trees are cut down
While the curved ones are left standing

Don't be too honest or ethical. Mostly, such good souls are taken for granted. By giving an analogy of straight trees, Chanakya advises us to be more practical in life.

Morally upright people

Chanakya says it is not always in your best interest to be unrealistically high-principled. Such high-minded people are not valued, and what's worse, they are even persecuted for being good. He gives the example of straight trees in the forest.

Curved trees are left alone

What happens to straight, tall trees in a forest? They are felled illegally. Because their wood is without bends and curves, they fetch high prices in the market; they are very valuable in the furniture trade. Also straight trees are easier to cut as opposed to twisted ones. So nobody touches gnarled trees. They are left alone and they live long. A straightforward, innocent person, not versed in the ways of the world, can be duped easily. On the other hand, street-smart and wily people know how to get out of trouble. So don't be too straightforward, says Chanakya. The lesson here is, don't harm others, but be ready to protect yourself.

11.9

Don't let your foot touch:
Fire, a teacher, a Brahmin,
A cow, a virgin,
An infant and an old person

Our culture gives the utmost importance to respecting others. For this reason, it is considered extremely impolite to touch someone with one's foot. It is the epitome of disrespect. Chanakya lists many people and objects one shouldn't touch with feet.

Fire, teacher, Brahmin and cow

Fire is sacred and the symbol of knowledge. Hindus worship Agni, the god of fire, and give him a place of pride at any auspicious event. He stands in as the universal witness to all good things, be it a wedding, a housewarming or the naming ceremony of an infant. So always respect fire. Likewise, a teacher should also be given respect. Anyone who imparts wisdom to you acquires a sacrosanct position in your life automatically. A Brahmin who performs sacred rituals and worships God is also a very dignified person. The cow is considered the mother, *Gomata*, because she gives milk. Don't disrespect the animal.

A virgin, an infant and old person

A virgin is the symbol of purity and chastity, so she should be given respect. A baby is considered equally pure, innocent and God's gift. An old person should not be disrespected owing to the experience he has gained over his lifetime. He symbolizes knowledge and experience. Touch his feet rather than touching him with your foot.

11.10

Infatuated, the foolish man believes
The charming lady is enamoured by him
He dances under her spell
Like an entertaining bird

A person who is under the spell of a beautiful woman will dance to her tunes. The foolish man believes that she is in love with him but in reality he is entertaining her with his antics.

An infatuated man

Who doesn't behave foolishly when in love? According to Chanakya, a man who thinks a beautiful woman is in love with him is being foolish. When in love, men lose the ability to think straight. Such a man will go to any length to please his ladylove.

Dances under her spell like a bird

No one wants to upset the object of their affection. Chanakya says unwise men become enchanted with a woman's beauty. Such a man behaves like an excited bird, dancing around his lover. He thinks she's in love with him, but in reality, she's just entertained by him. So be prudent and realistic in life; don't behave nonsensically in front of those you wish to impress. It will only amuse them and you will lose respect in their eyes.

11.11

He who befriends
An immoral, evil-minded,
Crooked and vicious man
Meets his ruin very quick

One should have friends but at the same time should be careful about who one is befriending. Be careful of bad company, for it can destroy you.

The immoral and the evil-minded

An unethical person cannot be trusted at all. Immoral thoughts and behaviour are the main causes of a man's downfall. Also don't acquaint yourself with a disreputable person. His malicious thoughts can affect you too. There is research that suggests that your behaviour will largely depend on the five people you closely interact with on a daily basis. So be careful who you associate with regularly.

The crooked and the vicious

Crooked people don't care for anyone but themselves. What's the point of being friends with a person who is not going to have your back in an emergency? And those who are vicious by nature should be kept at bay. They don't care who they attack, verbally or physically, when they are angry or annoyed. Such people are dangerous to be around.

11.12

**Vain is rain in the sea
Vain it is to burn a lamp in daylight
Vain is to donate to the rich
And vain is the food given to the one without an appetite**

Do not give a person something they already possess. What is the point in doing so? So choose to bestow gifts on those who need or deserve them.

Rain and the lamp

Rain is most needed in drought-affected areas. The sea already has enough water. In addition, when pure rainwater mingles with the salty seawater, it becomes impure to drink. So rain falling in the sea is useless. And so is a lamp lit during the day. There's ample natural light during daytime and it is therefore futile to use a lamp. The lamp is for the night when everything is drowned in darkness.

Donation and food

The rich by definition have money. They do not require donations. In fact, it is the rich who should donate their wealth to those who are less fortunate. Likewise, additional food is of no use to the person who has eaten well and satisfied. He cannot enjoy it at all.

11.13

Shaving at the barber's home,
Applying sandalwood paste or frankincense on a stone,
Seeing one's own reflection in water,
Deprives even Indra of his affluence

Always be aware of your stature in society and behave accordingly. Do not act mindlessly. If you do so, you will lose your reputation and become a laughing stock in society.

Shaving and stone

A barber's job is to shave men's beards and cut their hair. But there's no need to visit the barber's house for this service. In the olden days, people called the barber home to attend to their hair care needs. Today one can always go to a saloon to get the job done. Applying sandalwood and incense to a stone is also ridiculous. It's just a stone; it is no way sacred. Here Chanakya is ridiculing idol worship.

Reflection and Indra

Admiring one's own reflection in water is an act of vanity. Only one who is vain will keep admiring his own image. Even Indra, theking of gods, will be mocked for all these activities and stands to lose his place among the gods as a result.

11.14

Don't come in between
Two Brahmins, a Brahmin and the sacred fire,
A husband and his wife, a master and his servant
And a plough and an ox

Mind your own business. Don't poke your nose into something that is not relevant to you or you do not understand.

Two Brahmins and a Brahmin and his fire

When two wise people or elders are engaged in conversation, do not interfere. It is a sign of disrespect. And don't interfere when a Brahmin is performing holy rites in the presence of fire.

Husband and wife, master and servant, plough and ox

Never interfere in a couple's relationship, even if they're fighting. Marital discord is for the husband and wife to resolve. You will be doing them more harm than helping them by interfering. Never admonish or compliment another's servant. That's for his master to do. The one who pays the wage gets to mange the servant. A plough and an ox are also partners for life; one cannot function without the other. Understand that some bonds are long-term and you must respect that.

11.15

A poisonous snake, a king, a tiger,
A wasp, a tiny tot,
Another's dog and a fool
If found asleep, don't awaken them

Some like their sleep and do not like to be disturbed. They react viciously when awoken without notice. So it's better to let them snooze. Aren't they lucky!

A poisonous snake, a king and a tiger

A snake will not harm you if you do not disturb it. So why should you unnecessarily disturb a sleeping snake? Do you want it to bite you? The same goes for a king; he is powerful enough to imprison or even execute anyone who annoys him. This applies to anybody powerful. People in power can topple your world with their influence in an instant. So stay away from annoying such people. And who would even think of waking a sleeping tiger?

A wasp, a baby, a dog and a fool

A wasp sting is painful and poisonous. It's not an insect to meddle with. A baby takes a long time to settle down and sleep. If you disturb a sleeping baby, it will bring the house down with its cries. Also, a dog can be the friendliest animal. But if you're not the dog's master, don't disturb him while he is sleeping. He could attack you. A fool is no use awake, so why bother waking him? Let him sleep and you will be spared his foolishness.

11.16

Geese live wherever there's water
And go away when it dries up
Unlike the goose, a man should abstain
From coming and going as he pleases

Geese live close to water bodies; water is essential for their survival. They migrate even to faraway places in search of water. Unlike a bird, a man should settle down and live in a stable environment.

Geese and water

Geese are waterbirds. They are found near water bodies because fish are their primary food. They change their location based on seasons and the availability of water. They are migratory birds; here today, gone tomorrow. A goose doesn't have commitments and cannot be tied down to a place.

Don't come and go as you please

According to Chanakya, a man should have roots in one place; he shouldn't flitter about. He should have a family and he should be committed to his family. Men shouldn't live like birds; they shouldn't fly away during rough times in search of an easier life. There should be stability in a man's character, or else he is bound to fail. So don't abandon those who are loyal to you. Be faithful to your loves ones. This is the mark of a real man.

11.17

The pleasure-seeker should give up learning
A student should forsake revelry
For the pleasure-seeker can't attain knowledge
And a knowledge-seeker can't find happiness in revelry

The life of a person seeking sense gratification is completely different from the life of a student. The one who wants to enjoy a life immersed in pleasures cannot acquire knowledge. And the one who is serious about learning won't be interested in senseless merrymaking.

Pleasure seekers

Those who live to satisfy their senses are not interested in developing their minds. They live only to have a good time. Most people in this category will never value knowledge. Acquiring knowledge requires commitment and focus; one has to pursue it earnestly and single-mindedly. People who give importance to sense gratification should not bother with learning as they will not have the time or patience to undergo the hardships that make one wise.

Students

The goal of a student is to concentrate on his studies. He cannot waste his time having mindless fun all the time (small breaks are necessary). He should abstain from activities that will distract him from being disciplined—a necessary attribute of a good student. Therefore, Chanakya says a student should give up revelry and an extravagant lifestyle. Also, a true seeker of knowledge will not be interested in wanton merrymaking.

11.18

A student must completely give up these eight:
Lust, anger, greed,
Love for food, flashiness, excessive curiosity,
Too much sleep and too much servility

Continuing the previous train of thought on how to be a good student, Chanakya tells his students to avoid eight vices.

Lust, anger, greed and love for food

Lust is a distraction and an energy drainer for those who wish to learn. Anger makes one lose focus and creates unnecessary stress. Remember that when you're angry with someone, it's like drinking poison and wishing the object of your anger to die. And if you as a student are greedy, your mind will be caught up in satisfying that greed. Gluttony is also harmful because it will make you lethargic. Ever heard of anyone concentrating on his studies on full and satisfied stomach?

Flashiness, excessive curiosity, excess sleep and servility

Avoid showing off. Nobody gets impressed with flashiness. Learn to live a simple life, like a sage, and concentrate only on your studies. Don't be too curious either. Unnecessary curiosity can be a distraction. Excessive sleep makes a person lazy instead of refreshing him, so sleep only moderately. And servility or the excessive willingness to please others should be avoided. Don't give too much weight to other peoples' opinions. Concentrate on yourself and your studies; people will be automatically impressed when you score high marks.

11.19

A stupid person
Cannot be benefitted by direction
Despite the association with the Malay mountain
A bamboo does not turn into sandalwood

Someone's inherent nature cannot be altered, says Chanakya. Good advice is of no use to a stupid person, because he doesn't know how to make use of it. Likewise, in spite of being in the company of good people, a crooked person may not benefit at all.

Mindless person

A person who doesn't use his own intellect and powers of reasoning does not understand the value of good advice. Counseling him is like breaking your head to fashion a stone. The stone won't change form but surely you will have an opportunity to visit a doctor.

Bamboo and sandalwood

The Malay mountain range is mentioned in ancient Indian literature. It is one of the great mythical mountains of south India which has beautiful flora and fauna, especially sandalwood trees. This mountain range is home to bamboo, too. However, the bamboo does not turn into precious sandalwood even after being in proximity to these majestic trees. It remains as it is—hollow and without fragrance.

CHAPTER 12

———

LAST VERSES

12.1

O Rama, bless me with virtue,
Pleasing speech, a desire for performing charity,
Sincerity towards friends, humility towards teachers,
profound wisdom,
Moral purity, zeal for excellence, knowledge
of the scriptures,
Grace in appearance and reverence to Lord Shiva

Chanakya ends his final chapters with prayers. In his plea to Lord Rama, he requests a few blessings. If everyone asks for these blessings as well, their lives would be complete.

Good virtues, pleasant speech and a desire to perform charity

A righteous man is revered by all; good virtues shine bright even in the darkest of circumstances. Likewise, someone with pleasant speech spreads joy and warmth wherever he goes. He doesn't harbour enmity. Everybody likes to be associated with pleasant personalities. A desire to perform charity and help those in need is one of the most exhalted qualities a human being can hope to have.

Sincerity, humility, profound wisdom and moral purity

A person who is sincere friend is a real friend. Always ready to help, a friend in need is a friend indeed. Be humble in front of your teachers; they taught you all you know and the least you owe them is respect. Profound wisdom sets a man apart from his peers; he no longer craves for material possessions. Who doesn't want to be free of wants?

Zeal for excellence, knowledge of the scriptures, grace and devotion

One should strive for excellence; excellence should not be a goal, it should be the path itself. Knowledge of the scriptures and sacred writings of the great saints and sages will increase one's understanding of the world; they will make a person broad-minded. The ability to appear graceful under all circumstances is a great asset in navigating a life full of trials and tribulations. Above all, devotion plays a significant part in making the journey of life less tedious. So pray to God that your faith remains unwavering during turbulent times.

12.2

**Like an invitation to a feast delights the *Vipra*
Fresh grass makes a cow happy
A wife finds pleasure in being with a loving husband
O Krishna, the same way I rejoice in battle**

Chanakya here quotes from the *Bhagavad Gita*: Arjuna is speaking to Lord Krishna about his zeal for battles. Lord Krishna had guided Arjuna back into action when he felt disheartened about fighting and killing his own kin. In the battle field of Kurukshetra, when Arjuna was saddened by the reality of war, Krishna, through his sermon of the *Gita*, woke him up from lethargy and confusion and directed him to do his duty. Similarly, here too, Chanakya, after teaching us all his wisdom of *Chanakya Neeti*, is directing us into the field of action. Indian history is full of accomplished men and women who followed their calling and made a name for themselves. Our concept of spirituality is not about running away from the battles of life. In fact, our culture has created many men of action—the true *Karma Yogis*.

Invitation of feast to a *Vipra* and fresh grass to a cow

A Brahmin is usually delighted to attend feasts. Most Brahmin teachers live a frugal life and eat simple meals. So when they are invited to attend a banquet, they welcome the occassion—not only because of the food but also because they will get a chance to interact with the guests at the venue and spread their wisdom. And cows love grass, the greener the better. Left to graze on a good pasture, they find happiness and contentment in such a simple activity.

Wife with a loving husband and love for the battlefield

A wife's happiness is in being with her loving husband. Her joy knows no bounds when she gets to spend time with her beloved. Likewise, the great warrior Arjuna tells Krishna that he is the happiest when he is on the battlefield, when he is in the middle of all the action. A warrior's duty is to fight his adversities. So be a warrior in the face of challenges; be like the fearless Arjuna and the victory will be yours.

JAICO PUBLISHING HOUSE

Elevate Your Life. Transform Your World.

ESTABLISHED IN 1946, Jaico Publishing House is home to world-transforming authors such as Sri Sri Paramahansa Yogananda, Osho, The Dalai Lama, Sri Sri Ravi Shankar, Sadhguru, Robin Sharma, Deepak Chopra, Jack Canfield, Eknath Easwaran, Devdutt Pattanaik, Khushwant Singh, John Maxwell, Brian Tracy and Stephen Hawking.

Our late founder Mr. Jaman Shah first established Jaico as a book distribution company. Sensing that independence was around the corner, he aptly named his company Jaico ('Jai' means victory in Hindi). In order to service the significant demand for affordable books in a developing nation, Mr. Shah initiated Jaico's own publications. Jaico was India's first publisher of paperback books in the English language.

While self-help, religion and philosophy, mind/body/spirit, and business titles form the cornerstone of our non-fiction list, we publish an exciting range of travel, current affairs, biography, and popular science books as well. Our renewed focus on popular fiction is evident in our new titles by a host of fresh young talent from India and abroad. Jaico's recently established Translations Division translates selected English content into nine regional languages.

In addition to being a publisher and distributor of its own titles, Jaico is a major national distributor of books of leading international and Indian publishers. With its headquarters in Mumbai, Jaico has branches and sales offices in Ahmedabad, Bangalore, Bhopal, Chennai, Delhi, Hyderabad, Kolkata and Lucknow.

SINCE 1946

CPSIA information can be obtained
at www.ICGtesting.com
Printed in the USA
BVHW082325300721
612908BV00003B/220

9 789388 423571